ENTERPRISING EUROPE

ENTERPRISING EUROPE

A new model for global business

General Editor: Nick Isles

First published in 2002 by
Spiro Press
17–19 Rochester Row
London
SW1P 1LA
Telephone: +44 (0)870 400 1000

© Spiro Press 2002

ISBN 1 904298 18 4

British Library Cataloguing-in-Publication Data.
A catalogue record for this book is available from the British Library.

Library of Congress Cataloging-in-Publication Data on File.

The views expressed in this book are the authors' own and do not necessarily reflect
those of their organization or professional affiliation.

Spiro Press USA
3 Front Street, Suite 331
PO Box 338
Rollinsford NH 03869
USA

Typeset by: Wyvern 21 Ltd, Bristol
Printed in Great Britain by: The Cromwell Press
Cover design by: Cachet Creatives

Acknowledgements

This book would not have been written without the efforts, energy and enthusiasm of Marcello Palazzi. Marcello's network and contacts are, quite literally, global and it was he who first mooted the idea of holding a gathering (the European Enterprise Summit) of progressive European entrepreneurs and others, in London in November 2001. The vision of a renewed and reinvigorated Renaissance continent, capable of providing a better route map for the development of global capitalism, inspired the Enterprise Summit, organized by the Progressio Foundation, The Work Foundation (formerly The Industrial Society) and the State of the World Forum. And that summit inspired this book.

I should also pay tribute to Will Hutton. It was his recognition of the potential that exists in European economies to describe a better way of doing business that matched Marcello's vision and enthusiasm.

I'd also like to thank my colleagues at The Work Foundation, particularly Memuna Forna, for their support and encouragement in letting me take the time to organize the summit and then put this book together.

Finally, thanks also to Spiro Press for their support and guidance.

PROGRESSIO FOUNDATION (NL)

Progressio Foundation is in the business of *crafting strategic enterprise initiatives that advance human progress,* operating in the roles of think/do-tank, strategic connector and venture catalyst working in partnership with progressive entrepreneurs and leaders from the public, private and non-profit sectors.

Progressio's deliverables are:

- Agenda-setting events: global conferences, forums, round-tables and other key events that add to society's welfare.
- Business and civic projects: networks, alliances, special projects and ventures that integrate the interests of progressive businesses and society.
- Learning activities: selected publications and leadership and enterprise development programmes.

Over 80 projects in Europe, the USA, India and South America in partnerships with dozens of leading organizations for a monetary value of US$13 million – far greater if one considers its multiplier effect – have been successfully completed since 1989, when Progressio was founded by Marcello Palazzi, President, and Paul Kloppenborg, Chairman.

THE WORK FOUNDATION (FORMERLY THE INDUSTRIAL SOCIETY)

The Work Foundation is a wholly independent, not-for-profit body and holds Royal Charter status. Members include companies of every size, from every sector of the UK economy, along with public sector organizations, charities and trade unions.

The Work Foundation is committed to campaigning to make work better.

Its remit is to imagine, advocate and develop better ways of working. This means a commitment to progressive work practices that empower employees, focus on high-performance working and ensure sustainable profit making. The Work Foundation is a forum for non-vested interest employers, as well as a font of intellectual resource, campaigning vigour and, increasingly, through its consultancy offering, development at the level of the organization.

STATE OF THE WORLD FORUM

More than a decade after the fall of the Berlin Wall, the world community continues to struggle in its efforts to define and establish a more compassionate, just, non-violent and ecologically sustainable world order. With this challenge in mind, the State of the World Forum was founded with the explicit purpose of gathering together the creative genius of the human family, its elders and innovators, in a search for solutions to the critical challenges facing humanity in the 21st century.

What has emerged over the past seven years is a community of commitment representing nearly 6,000 extraordinary individuals, from more than 100 nations and from a wide spectrum of disciplines and professions. The Forum community is united by a unique matrix of shared values and ideas, which appear to describe the outlines of a new global development agenda and ethic. The transcultural principles underlying this emerging ethic seem to lead naturally to a more responsible, compassionate and collaborative vision for the development of human societies, as well as a powerful common evolutionary enterprise for our species. With this inspiring possibility clearly in view, the Forum now seeks to fully explicate this vision and build a robust and fully dimensionalized leadership community, dedicated to embodying and communicating the principles and practices essential to co-creating a better world for humanity and all living things.

About The Contributors

WENDY ALEXANDER

Wendy Alexander is the [former] Minister for Enterprise, Lifelong Learning and Transport in the Scottish Executive. She was previously an adviser to Donald Dewar, the first First Minister of the Scottish Executive, and helped draft the Scotland Act. Her first ministerial position was as Communities Minister with responsibility for housing, social policy and local government. Before entering politics she worked as a management consultant in Europe, the USA and Asia and holds degrees from Glasgow, Warwick and INSEAD in Paris.

TOM BENTLEY

Tom Bentley is Director of Demos, Britain's leading independent think-tank. A Demos researcher since 1995, in 1998 and 1999 he worked as a special adviser to David Blunkett, MP, British Secretary of State for Education and Employment. He returned to Demos to take up the Director's post in 1999.

He has been described as 'one of Britain's leading policy entrepreneurs' by the *Australian Financial Review*, and as 'one of four men who think for Britain' by the *Financial Times*. His work has been published in 14 countries.

He was born and educated in the East End of London and studied Politics, Philosophy and Economics at Oxford University. He is a trustee of the Roundhouse and the Community Action Network, and chairs the steering group of the Centres for Curiosity and Imagination project.

TOM CANNON

Tom is Chief Executive of RespectLondon (UK) Ltd and Managing Editor of the *New Academy Review*. Born in Liverpool, he is an international authority on business, leadership, entrepreneurship and corporate responsibility. He has visiting professorships at Kingston, Bradford, Northumbria and Middlesex universities. Earlier, he was Chief Executive of the Management Charter Initiative (MCI); Director of Manchester Business School; Professor of Business Management at Stirling University and founding Director of the Scottish Enterprise Foundation and the International Institute for Corporate Responsibility. Earlier appointments include Durham, Middlesex and Warwick universities and marketing management posts in consumer and industrial goods companies.

He has published over 20 books, most recently *The Ultimate Book of Business Breakthroughs* plus over a hundred academic and professional papers, a regular column in the *Guardian*, frequent broadcasts on TV and radio besides writing for 15 national and international newspapers and magazines.

His contact address is tom@new-academy-review.com

DIANE COYLE

Diane Coyle runs the independent consultancy Enlightenment Economics, and is a reporting panel member of the Competition Commission. She is the author of several critically acclaimed books on the 'new economy', the latest of which is *Paradoxes of Prosperity* which was published in 2001. She was the Economics Editor of the *Independent* from 1996 until 2001 when she left to establish her consultancy and to devote more time to her writing. She holds degrees from Oxford and Harvard.

BO EKMAN

Bo Ekman is Chairman of Nextwork and adviser to global corporations, international organizations and non-governmental organizations (NGOs). Nextwork is a Stockholm-based consultancy on business environment strategy and the design of changes processes.

JOHN ELKINGTON

SustainAbility (founded in 1987) see themselves as a hybrid – part management consultancy, part think-tank and part lobbying organization. John Elkington launched the idea of triple bottom line accounting in 1995. Their success is based on knowing how businesses think and act. So they influence *thinking* as well as *doing*. The organization is determined to stay small and employs 20 people of 10 nationalities.

KAJ EMBRÉN

RespectEurope was launched in Stockholm on 29 March 2000. The prime movers behind RespectEurope are the business leaders Anita and Gordon Roddick, communications consultant Kaj Embrén and the environmental consultant Per-Uno Alm.

The business intent of RespectEurope is to act as strategic advisers in enhancing corporate competitiveness, by developing socially and environmentally responsible brands. The prime activity is to support companies with strategic advice and core competence, and to assist in implementation by coaching processes of transformation.

HAZEL HENDERSON

A native of Bristol, UK, Hazel is a global futurist, evolutionary economist and author of *Beyond Globalization: shaping a sustainable global economy* (1999) and seven other books on sustainable development. She serves on the editorial boards of *Futures* (Elsevier, UK), *Foresight* (Cambridge, UK) and *Resurgence* (Devon, UK). Her editorials are syndicated by InterPress Service (Rome) to 400 newspapers in 27 languages.

Hazel is a fellow of the World Business Academy and the World Futures Studies Federation, and adviser to the Calvert Social Investment Fund (Washington, DC) with whom she is co-creating the Calvert-Henderson Quality of Life Indicators. She held the Horace Albright Chair at the University of California, Berkeley, and has served on committees of the National Academy of Engineering, the National Science Foundation and the US Office of Technology Assessment.

TONY HOSKINS

The Virtuous Circle (TVC) is a specialist social marketing consultancy, set up by Tony Hoskins in summer 2000. TVC includes experienced consultants as well as strategic partners such as the Centre for Science Education. Tony's background is in marketing and general management, with experience of both corporate and not-for-profit sectors.

WILL HUTTON

Will joined The Industrial Society as Chief Executive in 2000. Since then, he has diligently worked to move the Society from its more recent role as an organization primarily known for its training activities (1970s-1990s), towards becoming an organization that can most closely adhere to the ideals on which the Society was conceived in the 1920s – as a charity whose mission is to improve working life.

Will has seen the Society through the development and growth of the Futures and Policy departments, and most recently, the decision to sell the training business, change its name, and focus on activities that will make a high impact on the quality of working lives of the people of Britain and become The Work Foundation.

Will has written several books, the most well known being *The State We're In*, published in 1995, and *The World We're In* in 2002.

NICK ISLES

Nick is Head of Current Affairs at The Work Foundation. His brief includes European Affairs as well as UK public policy. He has written and been a regular contributor to the media on a wide range of work-related and labour market subjects including long-term unemployment, work organization and the future of work. He has previously run his own public affairs and communications consultancy and was for three years Director of Development at the Employment Policy Institute, an independent labour market think-tank.

PETER JOHNSTON

Peter is a senior official within the Information Society Directorate General of the European Commission. He is responsible, with others, for developing Europe's networking and information infrastructure to enable the EU to become the world's leading developer of the potential of the 'new' economy.

ELISABETH LAVILLE

Utopies was created in 1993 by Catherine Gougnaud and Elisabeth Laville in order to promote social responsibility and help companies become more socially responsible in their everyday business. It was their belief that socially responsible business is more profitable and valuable, and that by building stronger links between all their stakeholders businesses create products that are more valuable and interesting to customers. Utopies encourages this through an extensive programme of education and by consulting with organizations about the delivery of Corporate Social Responsibility (CSR).

MARIA CATTAUI LIVANOS

Maria Cattaui Livanos has been Secretary General of the International Chamber of Commerce since 1996. As Chief Executive of the World Business Organization she is responsible for overseeing global policy formulation and representing the interests of world business to governments and international organizations. She was previously Managing Director of the World Economic Forum (WEF).

MARC LUYCKX

Marc lives in Brussels. He has studied mathematics and philosophy and has a PhD in Russian and Greek Theology. He has lived in Italy, Brazil and the US, and has lectured in Brazil and the US.

From 1990 until 1999 he worked directly for Presidents of the European Commission, Jacques Delors and Jacques Santer, as a member of the Forward Studies Unit in the European Commission. He has been one of the organizers of the EU programme called 'The Soul of Europe', and organized many meetings between President Delors and religious leaders, philosophers etc.

He is now active in futurology research and is Director of Vision 2020, a think-tank on the New Paradigm in Brussels.

ED MAYO

The New Economics Foundation works for a new model of wealth creation, which is human in scale, socially inclusive and ecologically sustainable. The Foundation is leading the UK debate on new models of socially-orientated enterprise, including:

- Show-casing successful inner-city enterprise through the Inner City 100 project.
- Developing policy for a 'mutual state', in which social entrepreneurs run public services, being accountable to direct stakeholders.
- Developing a new policy agenda for Corporate Social Responsibility, for example based on work pioneered by the New Economics Foundation – a radical social, economic and environmental affairs think-tank and research consultancy – on disclosure and social reporting.
- Developing policy for enterprise-led regeneration, such as the ground-breaking 'community investment tax credit' designed to create incentives for £1 billion of private sector investment in inner-city renewal.

For more information please visit www.neweconomics.org

ROBERT AG MONKS

Robert Monks is the founder of Institutional Shareholder Services, the world's leading corporate governance consultancy, and is the world's leading shareholder activist. In 1992 he founded the investment fund LENS which has developed the institutional activist method of investment. In 1998 he founded a similar organization, Hermes LENS asset management company, in the UK. He is a graduate of Harvard, Cambridge and Harvard Law School. He served as Administrator of the Office of Pension and Welfare Benefit Programs as well as sitting on the board of ten large private sector corporations.

GEOFF MULGAN

Geoff is head of the Prime Minister's Forward Strategy Unit and Director of the Performance and Innovation Unit in the Cabinet Office. Before that he worked for the Prime Minister as a special adviser on social policy issues, having previously been founder and Director of the think-tank Demos. Prior to that he worked in a range of roles as an academic researcher, consultant, a local government officer and an investment executive. He has also been a TV and radio presenter and newspaper columnist.

MARCELLO PALAZZI

Marcello is a business and social entrepreneur by profession who started his first company in environmental diagnostics at 23 and sold it at 33. He is founder President, Progressio Foundation ('Progress through Enterprise'), a catalyst, connector and do-tank delivering agenda-setting events, civic initiatives, social ventures and learning activities which was founded in Rotterdam in 1989 by Marcello, Dr Paul Kloppenborg and Professor Pjotr Hesseling.

Marcello is Co-chair of the State of the World Forum Europe, co-founder, Chair and CEO of HUMANICA PLC, a social venture company, London; co-founder of Galileo & Partners, a strategic philanthropy alliance; co-founder and co-director of Spirit in Business Inc and Spirit in Business Europe Foundation. He is also on the advisory boards of the Copenhagen Centre, Transparency International, Berlin, and non-executive director of eziba Inc in New York and Via3 Ltd in London. See www.progressio.org.

JOHN PHILPOTT

John was appointed Chief Economist at the Chartered Institute of Personnel and Development (CIPD) in November 2000. Prior to joining the CIPD he was, for 13 years, Director of the Employment Policy Institute (EPI), an independent policy think-tank. His research and publications have covered labour market trends, long-term unemployment, welfare-to-work, full employment, employability, productivity, minimum-wage setting, the euro and social Europe.

John is currently advising the European Commission on the impact of the European employment strategy.

ROBERT RUBINSTEIN

Robert Rubinstein is the founder and CEO of Brooklyn Bridge, the Triple P Performance Center – a competence and training centre for triple bottom line investing – and the 3P Academy. Brooklyn Bridge is a knowledge broker, which links all relevant parties to achieve a desired goal with respect to CSR.

Robert has been active in CSR for the past 20 years. During this time he has worked mainly in publishing, creating five different magazines. His last publication, *Source*, was a management magazine dealing exclusively with CSR. He has always tried to integrate the basic concept of leaving things in a better condition than when he started. This relates to social, environmental, financial and spiritual conditions. In addition, through Brooklyn Bridge, he actively arranges funding for large-scale sustainable projects.

COLIN TWEEDY

Colin Tweedy has been Chief Executive of Arts & Business – formerly the Association for Business Sponsorship of the Arts, ABSA – since 1983. Arts & Business is the largest organization of its type in the world – a not-for-profit company that brings together the cultural and commercial communities.

MARC VAN DER ERVE

Marc is a consultant, independent futurologist and author with a specialization in organizational development, leadership profiles and behavioural traits of interconnected environments.

He is also the founder of Evolution Management, a consulting firm with international executive search and transitional leadership services founded on stages of corporate adaptation and development.

He holds degrees from INSEAD, Tilburg University and RIT in the Netherlands.

KAJ VOETMANN AND LARS MORTENSEN

The Kaos Pilots was founded in 1991 by Uffe Elbaek as a new form of business school, which the practitioners describe as a way of understanding the many changes happening locally, nationally and globally. The founders believe traditional business schools have become too hidebound and golf-club like to respond to these changes. Students at the Pilots spend a third of their time working on improving their own 'inner pilots'. The curriculum merges theory and practice into an 'intelligence ecology'.

ANDREW WILSON

The Centre for Business and Society, which is part of Ashridge – the international business school based in the UK – is a leading authority on relations between the corporate sector, government and communities, with a particular emphasis on the changing role of business in society. The Centre provides a range of research, education and consulting services.

JEAN-PIERRE WORMS

The Laboratory of the Future is an international association with two goals. The first is to identify and select original and practical initiatives throughout the world that bring about advances in every walk of life including business, employment, health, housing, transport and education. The second is to invite businesses and local authorities to take these pioneering initiatives as models and help to build a 'liveable future'.

The Laboratory of the Future applies three criteria when validating existing initiatives or seeking new initiatives and helping to develop them:

- Individual autonomy: any initiative should foster independence and a sense of responsibility in all those involved.
- Interdependence: any initiative should take its human environment into account and help to further the interests of those not directly concerned.
- Sustainability: a project with potential for the future should display some reliably sustainable features such as a return on investment with a manageable level of risk; sound daily management; long-term consideration of the social and human dimension; and an economic rationale that respects the environment and conserves and enhances natural assets and heritage.

NICK WRIGHT

Financial services firm UBS Warburg, a business group of UBS AG, provides a full spectrum of products to corporate, institutional and individual clients globally. With headquarters in London, UBS Warburg employs over 37,000 people in 30 countries world-wide. Nick Wright worked as a derivatives trader for over ten years before becoming Director of Corporate Responsibility and Community Affairs for UBS Warburg.

SIMON ZADEK

The Institute of Social and Ethical Accountability is the pre-eminent international professional body supporting organizational account-ability and sustainable performance. AccountAbility provides its individual and organizational members with access to leading-edge tools and knowledge, on-going research programmes, practical training courses and professional qualifications. For more information, please visit www.AccountAbility.org.uk

Foreword

The European model for enterprise

Romano Prodi, President of the European Commission

Enterprise is a fundamental part of the fabric of our societies and we need to recognize that governments at all levels are no longer the sole actors. The involvement of other key decision-makers is essential. Since the mid-1990s, global institutions have agreed rules-based approaches to moderating global trade flows and managing economic needs. These changes and developments have created a dominant model of 'how to do business'.

Europe has the potential to become the world's leading economic power-house. The countries of the European Union (EU) contain over 376 million people, a hundred million more than the US. In 2000, it exported over 780 billion euros worth of goods, 110 billion more than the US. With the single market, competition rules, the single currency and common social and environmental values, I believe the EU has created an area that promotes economic growth, trade and social values. The establishment of the European Central Bank (ECB) and the single currency was one of the best ways to defend European enterprise against currency speculation and regain sovereignty over economic affairs. The EU can also reasonably claim to have developed strong policies over environmental and consumer protection, high levels of international assistance, the best trade preferences, good political dialogue and the most efficient co-operation with developing countries. In this way, we have begun to, and must continue to, promote a distinctively European model of enterprise.

The European model offers a new agenda and culture of enterprise, which encourages its creative, innovative, ethical, socially engaged, environ-mentally and culturally enriching dimensions.

In Europe, thousands of citizens, companies, workers, local authorities, civic bodies and governments have realized that a distinctive form of enterprise, a progressive European enterprise, meets that description. It is an enterprise agenda that draws on the best European traditions of social change, justice, equity, democracy, welfare, cultural-wealth creation and cultural diversity.

The core of the new European enterprise agenda is not a political construct. It is economic, practical and bottom-up as much as top-down. It is emerging from the diffusion and scaling up of the myriad well-tested policy innovations, good practices and new strategies already at work across Europe.

There is also an attempt to create a market approach that is geared to sustainability. It is about ensuring a better quality of life that combines ecological, social and economic concerns and offers business opportunities for companies that can improve the lives of the world's people.

Government needs to become leaner, more strategic and less bureaucratic. Evolved rather than imposed solutions need to be applied where appropriate. Entrepreneurialism needs to be encouraged wherever it is found and not hampered by protectionist attitudes or old-style regulation. Subsidiarity needs to be strengthened and local decision-making empowered. Ethical banking and investment standards need to become the norm, not the public-facing optional extra to attract customers while nothing much really changes underneath.

At the Lisbon Summit in 2000, the European Council meeting agreed a 10 year strategy aimed at lifting EU economic growth to an annual average of 3% and creating 20 million jobs in the region. The strategy of Lisbon is a response to both economic fundamentals and the Union's capacity to manage the transition to a knowledge-driven society. While the ultimate responsibility for improving competitiveness in Europe and for stimulating the growth needed to fund an inclusive society lies in the hands of businesses and individuals across the Union, public authorities at all levels, including the Union's institutions, have a role to play. They must create a policy framework within which innovation and change can occur. The Lisbon strategy points the way to long-term growth and more jobs.

This approach combines economic, social and environmental policy strands into a single integrated strategy spreading over a decade and as a result offers a degree of long-term stability.

The actions range from driving up employment and training rates across the Union to the detail of creating a single European sky, of measuring and tackling social exclusion, and of opening up financial markets in order to release the investment funds needed by public authorities and businesses.

The Lisbon strategy is much more than just a new way of working. It represents a balanced agenda which translates into pursuing macro-economic stability alongside micro-economic reforms, stimulating growth, opening markets and competition alongside public and private investment in human capital and social reforms. It uses a sound economy as a motor to invest and connect people, ideas, skills and finance within open global markets. The Lisbon strategy is a good means to promote a European model of entrepreneurialism.

And *Enterprising Europe*, in describing and discussing the elements of the European model, is an important landmark on the journey to building a progressive, entrepreneurial and just world. I commend it to you.

Contents

Introduction

Juan Somavia, Director General of the International Labour Organization (ILO)

This publication comes at a critical moment in time, as a global economic downturn and uncertainty about the pattern and direction of globalization combine to threaten the livelihood and security of millions of people and their families throughout the world.

Even before the events of 11 September 2001, the world was facing a major work deficit. In the course of the 1990s global unemployment grew from 100 to 160 million. It had grown to 190 million by the end of 2001. One billion people are unemployed, underemployed or working poor; and 80% of the working-age population do not have basic social protection. In many respects, poverty and widespread insecurity about the future is the chronic social ill of our times. Working people worry that their jobs may simply disappear tomorrow, swept away by market and financial forces over which they have no say and about which they have little understanding. Business people also find that their enterprises fall prey to external shocks they can neither predict nor resist. All this represents a major crisis in human security.

In order to tackle these social ills, we need to change the current direction of the global economy and craft a pattern of globalization that is built on equity and sustainability. It is clear that business must play a positive and responsible role to this end and has a direct stake in being an instrument of social progress. There are already many instances of this, ranging from social entrepreneurship to the need of rating agencies to incorporate the notion of social risk, and from socially responsible investment to fair trade campaigns.

There is both an economic and moral case for business engaging in the promotion of values and social goals in the global economy. Deregulation and privatization – integral elements of the global economy – are widely linked in the popular mind to a shift in power from the public to the private sphere. There is a sense that business is shaping society in totally new ways as the turnover of companies has come to dwarf the economies of many countries. A world that fails to close the poverty gap and promote social inclusion will become a world in which globalization will prove unsustainable and many traditional and emerging markets unstable. This places responsible business practice firmly at the centre of the global development agenda.

I believe that business needs to be actively engaged in the search for solutions to emerging problems alongside governments, labour and civil society. We need leaders who are prepared to break with old ideas and exercise intellectual and managerial leadership in order to fashion a new and different future. The ideas that are presented in *Enterprising Europe* go a long way towards achieving this future. They demonstrate that with the right policies the market can be steered to serve social and environmental ends. They also demonstrate that responsible business practice neither undermines enterprise nor denies the need for profit. Instead, the concern is to focus on how enterprise can make its impact on society positive and productive. In the final analysis – in any walk of life, whether for profit or not – it is creative and innovative entrepreneurship that makes the difference.

Europe is well placed to provide the political and economic leadership needed to meet the challenge of making globalization work for all. I warmly applaud and support this initiative to develop a progressive European enterprise strategy, as it will help to lay down the foundations of a much-improved system for the governance of globalization.

Overview

Building a new model for global business

Nick Isles, The Work Foundation, and Marcello Palazzi, Progressio Foundation

'Oui, c'est l'Europe, depuis l'Atlantique jusqu'a l'Oural, c'est l'Europe, c'est toute l'Europe, qui decidera du destin du monde.'

Charles de Gaulle, 23 November 1959

Following the events of 11 September 2001, it is clear that the conservative Bush administration in the United States has not led the world into a new era of internationalism. The attack on the World Trade Center and Pentagon have unleashed powerful emotions around the world – sympathy for the victims certainly but also a recognition that the West, and the US in particular, is disliked, loathed even. For some the hatred is born out of fanaticism. For others it is the knowledge of Cold War rivalry that encouraged civil war and despotism in too many places. And for others it is because of their knowledge of so many people's daily experience of an economic system – however loosely one describes such a system – that creates invidious inequalities of wealth and opportunity, where the many gain the least and the few, who already have most, gain more.

Whatever the reasons one factor stands out. Over the last decade, since the end of the Cold War, attention has been fixed on the development of what has been dubbed globalization. Economists and commentators may debate its extent or its 'newness' but all agree that the world has shrunk and is still shrinking; that international trade flows have increased dramatically; that, on the whole, the world has become more prosperous but that too many people are still living in poverty, unimaginable unless witnessed.

Since the mid-1990s the world has lived through major economic crises in East Asia, Russia and Mexico. It has seen the proportion of global GDP generated by sub-Saharan Africa actually fall and global institutions struggling to adapt to the task of providing an agreed rules-based approach to moderating global trade flows and managing economic needs.

Underpinning all these changes and developments has been a dominant economic model – developed by the conservative right in the US and UK – where shareholder value is the guiding mantra. As Will Hutton argues in his chapter, the exporting of the 'American Dream' has been based on a myth of the superiority of the US model – institutional, economic, societal – which is not rooted in fact.

Against such a backdrop the anti-globalization movement has become more vigorous and violent. Their solutions to the real and perceived injustices of the global trading regime range from autarky to anarchy. Yet there are other voices calling for change and reform. Voices that argue there are genuine alternatives to the current hegemony, alternatives that maximize the benefits of a market economy in a more just and equitable way. The world needs other paradigms, other models with which to compare, contrast and then construct those global institutions, cultures and customs that work for all nations and every sector of society within those nations. Hutton and many other contributors argue that Europe offers an alternative vision for the world community of 'how to do business'.

Hazel Henderson, in her contribution, shows why and how measuring progress differently will provide a key lever in changing the way business is done. While Geoff Mulgan (Director of the UK government's Performance and Innovation Unit) and Maria Cattaui Livanos (Secretary General of the International Chamber of Commerce) discuss from their perspectives the extent to which governments can and should deliver change.

This debate – the enterprise debate – is now forming the world's dominant agenda. It is the enterprise debate that is therefore the subject of this book.

ENTERPRISE IS NOW CENTRE STAGE

As enterprise has increasingly assumed centre stage – as an economic, social and political force – the need to lead and manage its powers for maximum public benefit is no longer optional. Yet too often the public good is seen as having little to do with the pursuit of profit.

In Europe, thousands of citizens, companies, workers, local authorities and civic bodies as well as governments have realized that a distinctive form of enterprise – a progressive European enterprise – meets that description. It is an enterprise agenda that draws on the best European traditions of social change, justice, equity, democracy, welfare, cultural-wealth creation and cultural diversity.

First some facts. As Romano Prodi says in his Foreword, Europe has the potential to become the world's leading economic power-house. The countries of the European Union contain over 376 million people, a hundred million more than the US. European GDP is around 8 trillion euros, only 725 billion euros less than the US. In 1999 it exported over 760 billion euros worth of goods, 110 billion more than the US and 360 billion more than Japan, leaving it with a trade deficit of only 16 billion euros and making it the world's dominant exporting region.[1]

And this is just the starting point. At the Lisbon Summit in 2000, the European Council meeting agreed a 10 year strategy aimed at lifting EU economic growth to an annual average of 3% and creating 20 million jobs in the region. The Barcelona Summit in March 2002 gave this process new impetus. Altogether it is a vision of growth and prosperity that is seductive.

But what does this vision look like in reality? Some of Europe's political leaders have been stating the case as they see it. Romano Prodi said (in a speech to the European Business Summit, 11 June 2000): 'There is, however, one risk no firm can afford to take if it is to remain profitable in the medium and long term: the risk of ignoring the changing awareness and expectations of Europe's citizens. Citizens as consumers still want best products at the best price. But recent developments have shown they want more than that.'

He continued: 'This "more" embraces ethical values, democracy and justice, as well as environmental concerns and – more generally – sustainable

---

[1] Eurostat

development. The kind of society Europe's citizens are calling for today involves new kinds of relationships between employers, employees, the State and the environment. It requires both public authorities and business to show a new sense of social and environmental responsibility.'

He concluded: 'The successful firms of tomorrow will be far-sighted and responsible enterprises that have responded to the demands of Europe's citizens as workers, as consumers, as investors and as inhabitants of their region and country, of Europe and of the world.'

This theme found echoes in the words of Antonio Guterres, Portugal's Prime Minister, in opening the Lisbon Council meeting: 'It is necessary to combine innovation with social inclusion.'

Lionel Jospin, the [former] French Prime Minister, also spoke in the same vein, in a speech on 28 May 2001. He said: 'Europe ... is first and foremost a work of the mind, a societal model, a world-view.'

He continued: 'In a world now globalized, our Europe cannot sit back as an island of relative prosperity and stability. To selfishly turn inward would be to fall victim to illusion and denial. Europe offers a model open to the world and particularly to the Mediterranean and its rim. Europe is called upon to point globalization in the direction of law and justice.'

Such values and practices need reinforcing given the events of the first half of 2002 in France and Holland. The rise of the neo-right is a symptom of the concerns of Europe's peoples about the uncertainties that globalization brings and the exact nature of further European enlargement and harmonization. Europe's economic models offer a vision of inclusivity and fairness that, combined with sensible policies on migration, can and must work for all.

However, the core of the new European enterprise agenda is emerging from the spread of many well-tested policy innovations, good practices and new strategies already at work across Europe. It is both theoretical and practical, ethical and innovative, creative and democratic. It is about ethics, integrity, leadership, accountability, innovation, creativity, 'culturedness' and good governance. It eschews old politics, interest-group democracy or sheer economic power.

The approach must be integrated (top-down as well as bottom-up), reflecting the needs and interests of wider society. And there must be a balance between thought and practice, long-term policy goals and short-term enterprise needs.

The agenda's building blocks, its foundations, include many interlinked issues. Indeed, it is the interlinking of these issues, the way they are mutually reinforcing and interdependent, that allows us to turn the vision into a reality.

In broad terms, expanded and expounded in what follows, the enterprise agenda encompasses at a minimum the following broad areas:

- social enterprise
- just economic policies that encourage innovation and entrepreneurship
- high ethical, environmental and human standards
- ethical investment funds
- access to micro-credit
- a public procurement programme that is sustainable
- a transaction regime that is transparent
- an ethical trading regime
- new forms of public interest companies.

ENTERPRISE REALITY

One of the new enterprise agenda's main strengths is the breadth of inter-related policy areas. For instance, connecting socially responsible investment to pension reform in the UK is likely to boost available funds for new firms offering sustainable technologies and services, a triple win for investors, enterprises and public interests.

The burgeoning interest in developing 'hard' Corporate Social Responsibility (CSR) measures is another example where government at all levels, business large and small, social partners, academia and civic society are all pulling in the same direction.

The European Commission is certainly taking this issue very seriously, building on the March 2000 European Council in Lisbon's appeal to companies' sense of social responsibility regarding best practices for lifelong learning, work organization, equal opportunities, social inclusion and sustainable development.[2]

The Union of Industrial and Employers' Confederations of Europe (UNICE) has also stressed that although profits may be the main goal of any company they are not the company's only *raison d'etre*.[3] Throughout Europe industries are contributing towards making CSR more than a reputation enhancing device. In Sweden, the office equipment industry has adopted a voluntary labelling scheme designed to develop more occupational and environmentally safe office equipment. In Holland, the Dutch Safety Contractors Checklist (SCC) aims to evaluate and certify occupational safety and health management systems of contractor companies.

The European Trade Union Confederation (ETUC) and European Centre of Enterprises made a joint proposal for a Charter for Services of General Interest in June 2000, designed to offer affordable prices for everyone for basic services such as basic banking. And the research community has demonstrated that socially responsible companies can attribute around half of any above average performance to their social responsibility.[4]

Part of, and linked to, the CSR debate is the attempt to create a market approach that is geared to sustainability. It is 'about ensuring a better quality of life for everyone, now and for generations to come ... Thus it combines ecological, social and economic concerns, and offers business opportunities for companies that can improve the lives of the world's people.'[5] As Dr Gro Harlem Brundtland, Director General of the World Health Organization, says: 'The real world of interlocked economic and ecological systems will not change; the policies and institutions concerned must.'

According to the World Business Council for Sustainable Development there are seven main keys to sustainability: through the market, innovation,

---

[2] Commission of the European Communities, Green Paper Promoting a European Framework for Corporate Social Responsibility, July 2001

[3] *Releasing Europe's Employment Potential: companies' views on European social policy beyond 2000*, UNICE

[4] *Industry Week*, 15 January 2001

[5] *Sustainability Through the Market* – World Business Council for Sustainable Development report

practising eco-efficiency, moving from stakeholder dialogues to partnerships for progress, informing and responding to consumer choice, improving market framework conditions, establishing the worth of earth and making the markets work for everyone.

Dr Olaf Kubler, President of the Swiss Federal Institute of Technology, claims this means a world of opportunity is now opening up: 'Sustainability does not mean turning the lights off and sitting in the dark with wool socks on … it's a strategy for progress that provides a good living today and an even better living tomorrow.'

In Denmark, the Novo Group offers an excellent role model for sustainability reporting. The Institute of State Authorized Public Accountants in Denmark and the Danish newspaper *Borsen* awarded the Novo Group the prize for 'Best Sustainability Report' for the 1999 Environmental and Social Report. The company now publish a separate annual environmental and social report. In the Netherlands, the National Environmental Policy Plan (NEPP) has improved environmental regulation by simplifying the permit process and encouraging voluntary covenants which allow government to set targets for the reduction of particular emissions, and industry to choose the best mix (technological, economic and planning) to achieve the result. One example of this in action is the Dutch Packaging Covenant.

CSR and sustainable business are just two areas where synergies are leading to win-win-win solutions. This is the aim of the European enterprise agenda.

EUROPE'S PROGRESSIVE ENTERPRISE AGENDA

In November 2001 over 80 of the world's leading thinkers, practitioners and political leaders gathered in London, UK, at the invitation of the Progressio Foundation and the then Industrial Society, to articulate the emerging progressive European enterprise agenda.

The London Summit was clear that throughout Europe all levels of society must demand, expect and stimulate responsible and sustainable enterprise both within their own borders, and globally, in order to drive forward such enterprise alongside progressive economic, fiscal and financial innovations that lead to wider societal welfare. Anything less, it was argued, would betray Europe's best traditions as the Renaissance continent.

The 'voice' of Europe world-wide needs to integrate the different activities of politicians and civil servants, progressive entrepreneurs, social activists, civil and civic actors, who provide a leadership example of what Europe stands for. Underpinning these arguments is an understanding that enterprise and entrepreneurialism are not the same as business. We need entrepreneurs in our public and voluntary sectors as much as in our private sectors. There is also a recognition of the role of culture in shaping the impact of entrepreneurs to innovate, create and effect change.

Enterprising Europe is aimed at all those interested in how business can work better. We hope business people, students, policy makers, politicians, academics and the media will want to read at least some parts of what follows. The book is structured as a journey from the global to the local, from the theoretical in sections 1 and 2 to the practical in 3 and 4, culminating in a draft agenda for a European progressive enterprise chapter – Appendix 4. It is a book about policy and a book about practice. Not all the contributors agree but the contents do reflect the latest thinking and development of progressive business practice. There has been some essential factual updating.

THE FUTURE

For over 2,000 years Europe has been the birthplace of so much progressive thought and action. From the demos of ancient Athens, through the 'What have the Romans done for us?' period of imperial domination and expansion. From the mercantilists of the late middle ages, to the parents of political economic thought, Rousseau, Mill, Smith, Ricardo and Marx. From the Renaissance to the Enlightenment to industrialization to the welfare state, Europe has been the cradle of innovation and enterprise. And today the story is no different. Globalization is not an immutable inevitability. It is a process capable of being shaped. It is the intention of those involved in developing Europe's progressive enterprise strategy to do just that.

SECTION 1
The Global Perspective

'The new electronic interdependence recreates the world in the image of a global village.'

The Gutenberg Galaxy, Marshall McLuhan, 1962

What Kind Of World Do We Want?

Will Hutton, The Work Foundation

Enterprise is like apple pie and motherhood. Nobody can contest its importance and virtue; we are all for it. Enterprise is the force for positive change. It is the ability to translate our imagination into reality – and it has been the force propelling western civilization since the dawn of modern times. It was enterprising mariners who opened up the globe; enterprising inventors who applied science and technology to create new machines and capabilities; enterprising workers who built trade unions; enterprising acts of government that built universal education and health systems – and of course enterprising businessmen who build great business organizations.

And this is the rub – the core of the argument that is at the heart of this book and animates its contributors. Over the last 25 years enterprise has been progressively narrowed in its conception to be defined solely as the act of business entrepreneurship – and entrepreneurship in turn has been defined as an individualist act. We have been taught to lionize the individual risk-taker who can see a market or technological opportunity and exploit it. Enterprise has come to be coterminous with individual business entrepreneurship in free markets – the gospel as preached by American conservatives and some of the ideologically driven members of the American business community, like Enron's former Chairman, Ken Lay.

We need to rescue enterprise from this trap, and recapture its original best conception. In the first place, enterprise is a much more subtle and sophisticated idea than simple-minded individualism. It is much more a social act embedded in social institutions and requires high social capabilities if it is to be successful. Great businesses are great organizations, and any organization worth its salt has to be rich in social capabilities and social capital. Thus even the narrow conception of enterprise as solely an individual business activity needs to be broadened to recognize that business too is a social affair.

And secondly, enterprise is a value and approach that is crucial and demonstrable in areas well beyond business; we need enterprise in government, in civil society, in the welfare state and almost every walk of life – just as each of these areas is a platform for enterprise. But we can only get the acceptance and dissemination of this enterprising quality if we recognize that enterprise is as subtle a concept as portrayed here – that it blends the individual's willingness to take risks and to venture with the social capabilities of the organization in which he or she finds himself as a worker or a manager. In this sense enterprise is socially produced and there are values and institutions that can support it to a greater or lesser degree.

This is not the view of American conservatives, and their rhetoric is unambiguous about what those values and institutions are. They are the American willingness to take individual risks aided and abetted by low taxation, great rewards and a refusal to condemn failure – instead seen as part of the learning process for any budding entrepreneur. Institutions get in the way of swashbuckling risk-taking. If a country or civilization wants more enterprise, then it must follow the American example – and so share in the great American success story of the last 20 years. High productivity. Enormous job generation. Low taxes. Labour market flexibility. And no insipid talk about social capabilities. That means regulation, which throttles enterprise.

It is this philosophy that needs to be taken on head to head. America works much less well than its propagandists insist, and Europe much better. Despite the brouhaha about the new economy etc, American productivity has grown slightly less if measured on a hourly basis than in Europe – 1.6% between 1991 and 1998 compared to 1.8% in Europe. Moreover, absolute output per man hour is higher in France, the old West Germany and Nordic countries than in the US. Where America scores is that it works more hours than Europe and more of its women work – but a readiness to work long hours to compensate for lower productivity and the proportional greater advance of the sexual revolution are not evidence of greater enterprise. Indeed, the Europeans, investing more and working smarter so they can work less hours to produce the same output as the Americans, are arguably the more enterprising.

Nor is high taxation associated with low growth; the high tax Nordic countries, Holland and France have all enjoyed rapid growth in both output and employment. Indeed there is little evidence that labour market regulation *per se* has damaged growth and productivity. Rather the European story over the last four decades has been one of narrowing the productivity gap with the US while sustaining better social outcomes. I believe these are fairer and more just societies than the US. There is, in short, a European model of enterprise that is distinct from the American – although, paradoxically, the best American companies are European in their approach.

And although there is much talk that Europe has given up on its model of enterprise and turned to the American, it hasn't happened. Europe, far from rejecting the values that underpin its societies and economies, has made great efforts to adjust and preserve them in the face of global pressures. These are the values that insist that institutions are social, that people must be valued – and that such principles must extend from business to the wider social contract.

European societies do not accept the American conception that private property rights and individual freedoms come before any assertion of a social contract. In Europe, private property comes with obligations to the wider community; in the US the opposite is true. This belief, enshrined within the US constitution and cemented in the interpretation of that constitution by the rulings of the Supreme Court, allows America to ignore up to half of its population.

If you're poor in America you're likely to stay poor. The welfare system works poorly in relieving poverty and the education system in promoting opportunity. On any measure of poverty reduction the US is out-performed by the Europeans – *en masse*. Or take health care. The US has an insurance-based system that costs around 14% of GDP and omits from its reach 43 million people or 16% of its population. Not surprisingly American life expectancy at 72.7 years for men is lower than that in the big four European countries, France, Germany, UK and Italy (average 74.2 years) whose spend on health care averages around 8% of GDP.

As for the much maligned European corporate sector, we have already reported the productivity figures. Companies are embedded in society and societal institutions such as the education system, transport system and local authorities. European companies – as do the best US companies – recognize these realities, pay their taxes and acknowledge the importance of this wider infrastructure. These companies do not exist apart from the societies that spawned them. They accept the legitimacy of the argument that calls for them to discharge corporate social responsibility, and try to take it seriously. They are public companies in the profoundest sense of the term.

All round Europe there are different means to achieve the same end – ensuring that businesses can sustain themselves as social organizations benefiting all their stakeholders and improving their social capabilities upon which competitive success hangs. In Germany, Austria and Holland, for example, representatives of the shareholding groups join representatives from the workforce and unions on supervisory boards that set the overall strategic direction of the company. Hostile takeovers are rare, so that industrial restructuring has to be agreed between consenting companies – the reason why so many mergers succeed in mainland Europe while they mainly fail in the US and Britain. Spain, Italy, France and the Nordic countries may have different institutions and mechanisms, but they arrive at the same end – while retaining their powerful welfare states.

Against such a background it is plainly wrong to think – as even many pro-Europeans do – that Europe needs slavishly to follow the American model of doing business. The US is not the economic masterpiece its propagandists claim it to be. In fact its success is based on very sandy soil indeed, propped up by some comforting myths ably exploited and extolled by its cultural industries.

The European model is distinct and valuable. European states must be helped to reform rather than repudiate their systems before the forces of globalization. Europe's commitment to the social is not a source of inefficiency but rather a source of competitive advantage; it is the core of a different conception of enterprise. As globalization increasingly takes an American hue, it is Europe's approach to enterprise that needs asserting, consolidating and disseminating. We need more enterprise, especially in those areas where it remains a dirty word – but if we are to make the idea respectable and genuinely constructive we need to rescue it from the attentions of its current champions.

Is There A New Power-Sharing In International Affairs?

Maria Cattaui Livanos, the
International Chamber of Commerce (ICC)

Is there a new power-sharing? Yes of course, but it might not be where you think, where or how you would like it to be, where newspapers and current mythologies would place it. There is a powerful litany being repeated everywhere today: 'Globalization has eroded the power of the sovereign state and its ability to govern.'

Is this true? Here are another two frequently asked questions:

- Is it reality or an illusion that globalization has transferred power from governments to business – and that, therefore, non-governmental organization (NGO) power is needed in order to 'control' or balance out the overweening strength of multinational (transnational) corporations?
- Do concepts of power-sharing confer a false status on business and NGOs, to which they really do not have a rightful claim since they are neither elected nor politically accountable?

Behind all this is the fundamental question so often expressed as: 'Who's in charge?' Or, if you wish: 'Do we have international structures commensurate with the needs of a global economy – and do we want them?'

Let's jump right in and look at government – actually, what we call 'the state' and the concept of sovereignty and the idea of control by the state over its affairs. Sovereignty was never as 'absolute' as we think. It has always been challenged. One has only to look at the relationship between the church and the state over hundreds of years. The Catholic Church was multinational. It would have been horrified to be categorized as an NGO, which it is today.

Sovereignty has never meant – in reality, in history – total, final, unshared authority. Contrary to the philosophers Thomas Hobbes and Jean Bodin (who are often credited with developing the idea of national sovereignty), today when we talk of sovereignty we don't mean absolute domestic order exercised by a single authority (which is what they meant by the nation state). We mean that states are able within their own boundaries independently to choose their own governments, to be free of intervention – internally.

What has happened in the world that we question this already not-so-absolute and not-so-historical idea of sovereignty? No doubt, you would say the advent of globalization.

Here again we get our history wrong. Globalization is far from new. We have seen previous phases of international business expansion, particularly during the latter part of the 19th century, which stopped fairly abruptly in the 1920s and 1930s with tragic consequences.

It is interesting that the last period of globalization was marked by cross-border trade, the free movement of capital and lots of emigration. The UK invested almost half its domestic savings abroad. The emerging markets of that period were Australia and Canada!

So, does this current process of globalization undermine state control as it has historically grown?

I maintain emphatically that it does not. Certainly not the reality of state control rather than somebody's imaginary idea of what sovereignty never was or has been. The problems posed by movements of information, goods, ideas and capital are simply not new. In fact, today, I believe the modern state is probably better equipped to respond. The Asian financial crisis was better handled and less devastating than the Depression.

What has changed? A major aspect is the authority and strength of the state – national governments – to put in place social welfare strategies that address the impact of international competition. For instance, states have strategies to develop higher skill levels for their workers to face changing pressures from international competition.

In many ways, the modern state has become considerably more effective in managing processes resulting from the flow of goods, capital and services. It is nonsense to say that national governments are unable to constrain powerful multinational corporations. Governments have ample and powerful coercive mechanisms at their disposal and we expect businesses to obey the laws, or bear the consequences. If governments can't manage this, it is they that are dysfunctional.

In fact, I maintain that the activities of the state have actually increased and have been extended in most countries and represent more, not less, economic power.

The myth of the erosion of government power is nonsense. Governments have immense power:

- to tax
- to spend
- to put social programmes in place
- to regulate economic activity
- to set up and implement judiciary authority
- to fine and to incarcerate.

Governments are and remain by far the most powerful players on the international stage – far more powerful than even the biggest multinational.

Just looking at the power to tax and spend is sufficient: if globalization were undermining governments, you would expect their spending power to fall. In the developed world, government activity in taxation and government expenditure have both increased as a percentage of national income since the 1950s.

In Canada alone, government spending rose from 28.6% of national output in 1960 to 45% in 1996. In that same period, far from diminishing, trade more than doubled as a share of national output.

Domestic welfare programmes everywhere have increased dramatically in the same or greater proportions as a nation increases its level of integration in the global economy.

Surveys fail to show any reduction in public welfare services as a result of globalization – the opposite, in fact. The higher the degree of openness, the higher the level of social security. In fact, if a country is to liberalize successfully, a certain level of social security is almost a pre-condition.

Failed globalization and public backlash can be attributed to weak state control, particularly over welfare services and market-regulatory or competition-regulatory systems. Where has the crisis of effective government programmes and authority been most acute? In states that are most isolated from the global economy, not states that are most integrated into it.

Effective, strong governments have evolved in this age of globalization as a new form of international power. Perhaps the most important aspect of a global economy combined with a global idea of sovereignty is that governments can sign on to any international agreements they choose – and they do so, more and more.

And it is here that we may be redefining our old concepts of the scope, obligations and duties of the state.

I would like to propose that globalization today means that sovereignty no longer needs to be defined as a nation state exercising independent individual control over all its cross-border movements. Instead, today's nation state can enter into contractual agreements to relinquish such control under agreed rules, while at the same time actively participating in shaping international politics and even international economic policies.

Thus, today there is a new sharing of power – but it is mainly among and between states, by mutual consent, as they adhere to agreements in so many areas. This process, of course, has been going on for many years but it has vastly accelerated recently and has gained in scope, drawing in more and more countries and also affecting everyday life.

For example, think of:

- air traffic control
- spectrum allocation

- IP treaties
- environmental conventions
- anti money laundering
- and, most importantly, financial stability measures and monetary policy.

This makes it even more crucial to assist developing countries, in order to ensure that they have the capacity to negotiate in these arenas. Entering such agreements is not a sign of weakness, but rather should be based on the strengths of the state to represent its peoples. Strong states are the best negotiators.

The second new kind of sharing of power is between governments and public scrutiny via the international market-place. There is no doubt that globalization subjects economic policies of the state to close and sometimes unforgiving scrutiny. You can either call this loss of economic autonomy or the true workings of global democratic economic supervision. If a government runs deficits for too long and builds up a crushing debt, investors may well flee. Certainly governments face pressure to control spending, inflation etc.

It is this discipline of the global market-place, perhaps, that gives rise to the idea that the multinational corporation is more powerful than government. Why does the global corporation seem so powerful when no company can impose taxes, set up a judicial system or have control over public security?

First of all, governments around the world have moved out of the business of business. On the whole, governments haven't become weaker by moving away from running individual businesses with proper regulation and competition structures. They still maintain their mandate to serve the broader public good. In fact, they probably do this better, with less conflict of interest. Today, the exceptions to the above occur in countries with the weakest economies and the least efficient and effective governments.

Secondly, business is the key engine of growth, of production, of employment and therefore of well-being. It is the aspect of people's daily lives with the greatest influence on their prosperity. Business therefore appears to have an enormous influence over everything.

If it isn't in the area of real power, it is probably in the sphere of influencing government that the greatest shifts are being seen. I maintain, however, that it is not just a semantic nicety to distinguish between the power of the state to act and to legislate, and the ability to influence.

The 18th-century French philosopher de Tocqueville described the power of public opinion in a democracy as the tyranny of public opinion. Now, with an increasingly sophisticated and comfortable citizenry around the world, 'public opinion' is exerted in an increasingly organized fashion, through civic groups and through targeted pressure.

In fact, this active citizenry considers itself to be knowledgeable on more and more issues and as an enhancer of the forces of democracy. In each of our democratic countries, we have structures and practices, rules and customs for just this sort of democratic expression, in order to handle the way in which different segments of the public exert influence.

But we have no such clarity of structures, rules and customs for exerting influence in the international arena.

Fundamental to various proposals of civic groups or NGOs is the search for an understanding and a reassurance as to the 'rules' by which a global economy plays. For many people, the complexities of a globalized economy are not understandable and not comforting.

I would like to conclude with some observations on this – on the perennial search for an answer to: 'Who's in charge? Who's in control?'

First, what do we want and expect from government today?

- a stable political system
- striving for the common good
- balancing competing demands
- a sufficiently comprehensive, transparent and non-discriminatory legal system
- making that framework work
- sound macro-economic fiscal and monetary policies
- rising standards of education, of health care, of social infrastructure – of quality of life.

Second, what is expected of business today?

- to create wealth and jobs
- support the common good and spread the wealth by paying taxes
- stimulate growth by investing
- be fair to shareholders, employees and the communities in which it operates
- take into account all those who feel it has an impact on their lives.

Business is most productive where the rules are clear and appropriate for a competitive international market-place.

That is exactly where the difficulties arise, because rules-writing/control is no longer monolithic and we have to live with complexity. For the moment, economic management is maintained and exercised by:

- national governments, as mentioned (first and most powerful)
- international agreements entered into by national governments (like trade agreements)
- self-regulatory mechanisms (not to be scoffed at since ICC is living proof that they can work)
- public and consumer scrutiny.

For business, it is clear that there is a continually increasing complexity of national, regional and international rules to which it is held accountable, with every day seeing further layers of regulation – ranging from food safety standards to financial transparency.

One of the most difficult challenges we all face is getting the balance right between rules and freedom. Our globalized world works best within mutually agreed rules, which, however, cannot be allowed to stifle innovation, risk and expression.

Since companies and governments are both rules-based, they can develop relationships in well defined areas. The same is true for trade unions. But what about other NGOs?

I would like to propose that any entity that does not enter into a framework of responsibility and accountability for its words and actions, and is not governed by clear and understood rules, will never have any real power or even long-lasting influence.

Thus, when we look at power-sharing in a global economy, it makes no sense unless we have agreed upon structures inside of which government, business and NGOs can relate to each other. Otherwise, all the rest is merely talk.

The question concerns the extent to which we need or want such systems and structures of what is now called global governance.

The global economy is probably less organized than we realize, with few good examples of global governance systems. There is no international central bank or global Federal Drug Administration (FDA) to certify that our drugs are safe and our financial transactions clear. The economic world is largely run by an accumulation of consensual practices and very few international rules.

In the search for how these rules could evolve, we might consider the following principles:

1. Globalization calls for even stronger state structures. It increases the cost of weak or incompetent government.
2. Globalization encourages cross-border co-operation among governments – particularly through multinational institutions and agreements.
3. If we develop rules that must be observed by national players and the global economy, then we need strong institutions to apply these rules. Think of international trade or global financial markets.
4. In addition to the formal power of established institutions, there is likely to be more and more resolution of issues through co-operation among governments in order to apply generally accepted approaches. Think of common standards evolving for supervisory authorities, which are sharing their knowledge and experience with counterparts from other countries.

In conclusion:

- Real power in the political, judicial, fiscal and military sense remains firmly in the hands of the state.

- Power can't be shared just because someone feels it should be.
- Power can only be shared where it is legitimately given within a set of agreed rules. It is thus being shared more and more among and between accountable governments (ie strong, responsible, competent and effective states). But the players who have an influence on those rules are evolving and include an increasing number of voices.
- We are also seeing the need for sets of good practices and agreed principles for those who would like to influence public opinion and governance structures.
- It is hard work influencing governments within the structure of a democracy. But let's not equate or mix up power with influence, or influence with vandalism.
- As always, changing or making the rules of the game is based on consensus and comes from within societies. Ultimately, it relies on leadership and political willingness to be innovative, to inform and to mobilize opinion.

SECTION 2

Change, Society And Enterprise

'Change is not made without inconvenience.'

Samuel Johnson, 1755

3

Complexity, Entrepreneurship And Self-Organization

Tom Bentley, Demos

Can the dynamism and diversity of an enterprise culture be reconciled with equity, social inclusion and a rich quality of life? The goal is not just to stimulate prosperity across a diverse collection of national economies, or even to establish the European Union as an alternative pole of growth in a regionalized world economy. Neither is it simply to preserve European traditions and institutions in a new and competitive global context. Instead, the goal is to establish forms of social and institutional order which enable the growth of sustainable prosperity alongside openness to cultural exchange and social diversity. This depends on the possibility of harnessing entrepreneurship and organizational innovation for the purposes of social sustainability and institutional renewal, rather than just as a force encouraging more competitive firms.

This chapter argues that a European enterprise agenda does not have to follow the logic of pure free market competition, or to accept that the price of ongoing prosperity is abandoning a concern for social cohesion and collective quality of life. But the direction of long-term change increasingly calls for a reinvention of governance and public institutions, and the reduction of dependence on command and control as a source of order in a complex, unpredictable environment. Shaping progressive responses to globalization and structural change depends on mobilizing the potential of Europeans as citizens, and on using institutional innovation to create systems of *self-governance* that can reconcile radical diversity and mobility with an underlying sense of coherence and collective purpose. Forging such systems will require a degree of political bravery and a long period of institution building through trial and error.

Europeans have gradually come to recognize the necessity of responding to the underlying forces that are restructuring firms, families and other social institutions. But there is still ambivalence in most national debates about the extent to which globalization should be allowed to impinge on the expectations and ways of life enjoyed during the post-war period. The clearest indicator of this unease is the sharpness of controversy over immigration in most European states. There is also an ongoing, and linked, debate about how far economic restructuring should be accompanied by a growth in economic insecurity and inequality for those at the margins.

Public appetite for state intervention remains equivocal, a product of conflicting forces within and between societies. The growing force of technological, economic and social change fuels the desire for politics that soften the edges of capitalism and enable individuals to thrive in a more open, fluid society. Interest in political issues has not waned, even where engagement with formal politics has done. Concern about the power of corporations, the quality of public services and the protection of the environment remains high. Such issues encourage the demand for governments to act. Simultaneously, though, the cultural forces of individualization and consumerism continue to fragment the traditional bases of social solidarity. Trust in public institutions and government, and willingness to vote, is still declining steadily in most countries.

In this environment, politicians and civic leaders have sought pragmatic, piecemeal solutions to the challenges of economic and social disruption. The election of social democratic governments in many parts of Europe during the late 1990s saw a renewed interest in active government, but all saw the necessity of allying themselves with the innovation and dynamism of new technology while also promoting social cohesion. Lionel Jospin's invocation of '*Oui*' to a market economy, '*Non*' to a market society captures the aspiration perfectly. But economic change and European politics have become more volatile in recent years. The prospect of global recession and the struggles of the single currency have sharpened disputes between

European nations and between interest groups about their relative needs. The Irish rejection of the Nice treaty, the election of an explicitly anti-immigrant government in Denmark, Le Pen's comparative success in the French Presidential elections and Pim Fortuyn's seismic effect on the recent Dutch elections (despite his death) are indicators of disquiet and anxiety among domestic populations. The violence of Gothenburg and Genoa demonstrated the rise of new and radically different challenges to the legitimacy of European leadership.

Governments and reformers are still struggling to find effective and legitimate institutional bases in a social and political environment characterized by uncertainty, fluidity and complexity. They are concerned to associate themselves with modernity, with the comfortable self-confidence of consumerism, the cultural openness and social diversity of city life, the dynamism of successful entrepreneurship. Freedom and mobility are habits that many Europeans are firmly wedded to, even where the value of personal choice includes social and ethical responsibility. But the consequences of unfettered liberalization are uncomfortable.

The danger is that a simultaneous concern for economic dynamism and social cohesion translates into contradictory tendencies; on the one hand a commitment to liberalization and rapid economic restructuring, on the other a defensive reinforcement of traditional public institutions. Such a strategy is ultimately self-defeating; economic and technological change are always accompanied by cultural and institutional change. Moreover, the long-term benefits of the 'new economy' depend on the creation of new, supportive public infrastructures, which are heavily dependent on public investment, if not on direct central provision. The challenge is to shape social movements and public institutions using principles that run with the grain of the new, fluid and network-based environment. There are many avenues towards such system building, but they rest on getting the right understanding of how historical change occurs, and how it can be shaped.

COMPLEXITY AND DISORDER: THE EDGE OF CHAOS

Long-term structural change causes disruption, vulnerability and loss as well as creating openness, diversity and wealth. Perhaps most of all it challenges established institutions and their methods of organization. The dramatic rise in the salience of international terrorism and world-wide economic insecurity during 2001 have added to the volatility of this mix. They have strengthened the recognition that collapse and disorder on a mass scale are real possibilities, and that many of the systems on which modern societies rely are on the 'edge of chaos', pushed relatively easily into extreme disorder and breakdown.

A defining characteristic of change in this wider environment is complexity. This claim is not new; it crops up regularly in the history of social thought, often in response to the disruption of technological change. However, the combination of rapid increases in the volume and complexity of formal knowledge, especially in science, and the flowering of new, network-based forms of communication and interdependence, or 'connexity',[1] provides good reason for thinking that the current period of change is special, if not completely unprecedented.

One primary impact of information and communications technology is to increase the volume and complexity of social and institutional interactions, as well as the degree of specialist knowledge used in economy and society. The ongoing progress of individualism and social diversity contribute further to, and are fuelled by, this phenomenon. The growth of personal freedom drives an ever-growing array of social and institutional arrangements and continues to undermine the categories of class, religion and family type. Globalization of economic exchange, communications and culture through interconnected technology networks contributes further.

The challenge for reformers is not just to find ways of understanding and interpreting these new forms of complexity. It is to shape them in purposeful ways. The most important dimension of this challenge is institutional; the massive, historically rooted systems of organization through which resources are allocated, needs met and identities forged. Institutions are not just convenient or rational ways of organizing large-scale activity. They are also an expression of, and an influence on, values. Modern organizations

---

[1] Mulgan, G, *Connexity: how to live in a connected world*, Chatto and Windus, London, 1997

are a response to the need for human activity to be ordered and carried out at scale. But during periods of rapid change, organizations also need to operate at the 'edge of chaos' in order to thrive.

The agenda and central concepts of the neo-liberal revolution were organized around one institution: the market. Market exchange was taken not just as the expression of individual sovereignty and rationality, but also as the most effective way to reconcile the growing diversity and complexity of human preferences. The most important element of the critique levelled at state socialism by the Austrian economist Hayek and others was epistemological – that markets offered the only possible way to make decisions about resource allocation that draw on the best possible knowledge, both about the structure of demand and about the relative merits of different supply options; in this view, the results of market competition stood as a final arbiter of value.

While recent years have seen a swing away from these purer forms of market liberalism, and a recognition that the underpinning resources that make market exchange possible also need to be actively renewed, we have become concerned again with how to cope with the collective consequences of billions of individual choices and interactions: traffic congestion, material waste, the hostility and insecurity of public spaces, the exploitation and marginalization of casualized labour markets, population movements etc. In all these cases, the challenge is the same: to find ways of coping with the indirect systemic effects of free individual choices which are not directed by any overarching form of social purpose, as channelled through the rules and decisions of collective institutions.

But the institutions that have, historically, provided countervailing power against the market have relied on a particular set of organizational principles: command and control. These principles have structured institutions including armies, empires, monarchies, government administrations, churches, modern trade unions and multinational corporations. They are a central feature of organizational life, not just in the 21st century, but throughout much of history.

The core principles are fairly simple: hierarchical distribution of authority and decision-making power, centralized control of resources and a vertical division of labour according to function and specialization. Within these systems obedience, loyalty and respect for rank are treated as virtues, and membership of the whole is closely guarded against outsiders. In government, two features also stand out: the formation of policy as a centrally determined objective which is then implemented in a rational and mechanistic way by setting rules and allocating resources, and the principle of vertical accountability – that final responsibility for decisions and financial allocations can be traced upwards from the point of implementation through a chain of command.

The combined changes of the last 50 years have seen a crumbling of hierarchical institutional authority. But the use of command and control principles to structure institutional life has lived on. And the result is that all, or most, of the institutions that follow these principles have seen their authority and their practical control steadily eroded. Hierarchical organizations are less able to shape, understand or respond to discontinuous, unpredictable change.

NETWORKS AND ENTREPRENEURS

One source of hope in this environment is that the creative power of entrepreneurship can be applied more broadly than just to the commercial arena; that entrepreneurial responses might provide solutions to social, civic and environmental challenges as well. The growth of pioneering, often business-led, initiatives and small-scale partnerships for change across Europe, from ethical financial investment to community regeneration, can provide the basis for further reaching, longer-term solutions.

However, harnessing the power of enterprise presents a challenge: bringing together many and diverse efforts, and promoting them across whole systems of activity in ways that do not undermine their dynamism or creative value.

There is, at least in theory, a mode of organization that provides an appropriate way to achieve coherence out of complexity. As Manuell Castells, the US-based Professor of Sociology, puts it: 'as a historical trend, dominant functions and processes are increasingly organized around networks.' Networks are increasingly seen as a source of prosperity through the development of new industries and the linkages of trade; as an underpinning for social cohesion and civic identity, through informal bonds of trust and collaboration; and as a way of co-ordinating and shaping large-scale activity without imposing rigid hierarchy on it. Networks provide an architecture through which rapidly growing flows of information can be managed and shaped, and a rationale for combining radical diversity with membership of some kind of unifying whole. Their promise is that 'A network-based social structure is a highly dynamic, open system, susceptible to innovating without threatening its balance.'

But efforts to build 'network governance' are still in their infancy. The internet has generated some attempts to set the rules and govern the common standards and protocols that underpin the virtual world. In some areas of global industry, groups of firms have come together voluntarily to promote voluntary codes of self-governance, for example on environmental and labour standards, as a response to consumer or media pressure which seeks to avoid statutory or regulatory intervention by the state. Efforts to link small-scale innovation or entrepreneurship in the social and civic fields, in order to increase their impact and their shaping effect on big institutional frameworks, are still highly limited.

The question, therefore, is whether the emergence of network-based forms of governance, which distribute responsibility and innovative potential widely across diverse fields of practice, can be built systematically out of the chaos and flux of the current environment. One starting point for answering this question is a better understanding of the process of change, which leads to successful institutional adaptation.

In many, though not all, respects social and institutional change can be seen as an evolutionary process. The goals of such change are open to democratic debate. In seeking to stimulate and influence such change, the underlying goal of co-ordination and political intervention should be seen as developing or supporting systems of *self-governance*.

EVOLUTION AND SELF-ORGANIZATION

Consider the way in which the struggle for organizational renewal is increasingly characterized: that of a struggle successfully to adapt to changes in the wider environment that present new threats and opportunities, including new rivals, where the environment is characterized by unpredictability, diversity and openness. In this characterization, the process by which organizations seek to adapt, survive and thrive looks remarkably similar to that of natural evolution.

Large organizations themselves act as systems that are more complex than their formal design, structures of control or legal definition allow. As they become more specialized and information-intensive, they look less and less like machines designed for specific purposes and controlled by central instructions, and more like complex sets of relationships between many different agents and sub-systems linked together in myriad, uncontrollable ways. If we were to view efforts at institutional renewal through a Darwinian lens, what would they look like?

First, the process of change is long and drawn out, and successful adaptation often arises from a series of unsuccessful attempts.

Second, perhaps we should view firms, unions, schools and public agencies not just as part of one single monolithic system, but as populations of agents with the same underlying characteristics seeking to thrive in their own local environment. This allows us to recognize that they are struggling to cope with complexity and diversity in their own environments, as well as with increases in the expectations of the formal governance systems that supposedly control their actions. Enabling such organizations to communicate with each other, and to learn from the efforts of others by building knowledge-sharing networks which span their local environments, may therefore make more sense than trying to devise new rules or management formulas that can generalize the solutions.

Third, the 'agents' making up these populations are, at least partly, autonomous; they have their own goals, routines and impulses, and are not waiting inertly for the latest batch of instructions from the centre, like a set of obedient gears or processing chips. This is one reason why the metaphor of 'levers' of power is so often inappropriate: while the tops of public institutional hierarchies are still often laid out as a set of commands over different functions, they rarely work as such in practice; ministers and chief executives might pull levers, but they are rarely certain what the outcome will be or when it will appear, and the detailed workings of the machine often remain a mystery, even to those most involved.

Fourth, destruction is as important as creation. In nature, death and decay is directly bound up in the release of resources for new attempts at life. As the economist Joseph Schumpeter recognized, the process of 'creative destruction' is an essential element in the cycle of renewal and adaptation followed by capitalism. Yet in the field of government and other non-profit organizations, there is little systematic pressure to integrate innovation decisively into the workings of the rest of the system and clear away old routines that have lost their purpose or value. Too often, attempts at innovation build shakily on what is already there. This is not necessarily an argument for introducing competitive markets into every field, but it does raise the question of how old forms of organization can give way to new in non-commercial spheres.

Fifth, evolutionary change advances by trial and error. The system cannot find out how well a particular variation or adaptation works without testing it in practice, and the extent of variation and experimentation partly depends on the extremity of conditions in the environment. Specific adaptations may not be particularly meaningful to the individual agent, but in the context of the whole population, they constitute the way in which it finds out how to go forward. This is also true of efforts to make organizations work better, but is not widely recognized. Wide variation in practice and systematic testing of new ideas and possibilities is therefore necessary for the possibility of sustained or radical improvement; hospitals do it with new drugs, but not with alternative working practices, for example. Even where variation and innovation are encouraged, there is often little systematic capacity for the whole system to learn from and adapt to specific innovations achieved by one agent within the population.

Few institutions are good at this kind of learning, and they are most often in the private sector. Designing and developing learning strategies for networks of entrepreneurial organizations, in any sector, is therefore a major and urgent task.

But there is a central difference between natural evolution and organizational life: that of moral purpose. Evolution is amoral: the central impulse of all living beings and species is towards survival through adaptation; there is no need to scrutinize or debate the underlying values and purposes of the exercise. This may be why, in the past, evolutionary metaphors have been so attractive to political thinkers wedded to free markets – the image overlaps with the myth of market neutrality and the ideal of perfect 'survival of the fittest' economic competition, in which the institutional framework does not have to arbitrate between the value of the competing projects since the process of market clearing and competitive destruction already does the job. One of the achievements of more recent evolutionary studies has been to identify the tendency of many species towards spontaneously collaborative and self-sacrificing behaviour in social groups, and the insight that successful species or populations always develop a balance between competition and collaboration which sustains their overall project.

This is why the process of institutional renewal depends partly on establishing common purposes around which organizations and citizens can rally. Sustainable organizational change has to harness not just the knowledge and information distributed across increasingly fluid environments, but also the underlying goals and motivations of the agents. This requires forms of organizational praxis in which the specific efforts of sub-systems and practitioners are informed by, and in turn help to shape, the rationale and functioning of the whole system of which they are a part.

There is, however, one overarching goal which might become a general focus for efforts to renew and reinvent our institutions. The study of complex systems is not solely the preserve of biological evolution: it comes from a range of disciplines including earth sciences and ecology, computer science and information theory, population studies and so on. All share the search for underlying organizing principles in complex, decentred systems where change is driven by diverse forces and causes unpredictable outcomes. Alongside the tendency towards systematic adaptation, another feature stands out: the impulse of many natural and human systems towards *self-organization*. Perhaps the clearest illustration is James Lovelock's Gaia hypothesis, which suggests that all life on earth is part of a single, indivisible, self-regulating system acting to preserve the conditions that make life possible.[2]

Other expressions of the idea of self-organization, notably Stuart Kauffman's, go further. Kauffman takes the fact that all living systems maintain coherence amid disequlibrium, that is by thriving amid unpredictable surroundings, and advances the hypothesis that 'on many fronts, life evolves towards a regime which is poised between order and chaos ... Networks in the regime near the edge of chaos ... appear best able to co-ordinate complex activities and best able to evolve as well.'[3]

This kind of lateral step – from the study of emergent forms of order in nature, to the possibility that complex, uncontrollable organizational interactions might form the basis of coherent self-sustaining systems – helps to strengthen the hope that common social goals and values can be actively renewed even while traditional forms of order continue to be eroded. The entrepreneurial behaviour of autonomous organizations can, potentially, be incorporated into wider systems of self-organization that can meet complex needs in systematic ways. The principle of complex self-organization may also provide a contemporary fit with the ancient democratic ideal of self-government.

AREAS FOR EXPERIMENTATION

This chapter has tried to sketch out a basis for conceptualizing systems of co-ordination and governance that thrive on complexity, diversity and entrepreneurship. It does not lend itself to immediate prescriptions; in fact, it suggests that successful policies will rest on practical solutions that emerge over time rather than being dreamed up and written down in think-tanks.

[2] Midgley, M, *Gaia: the next big idea*, Demos, London, 2001
[3] Kauffman, S, *At Home in the Universe: the search for laws of self-organization and complexity*, OUP, 1995

But there are a number of areas where an evolutionary approach might help to shape, or accelerate, an agenda for renewal:

- Innovation strategies for the 'new' economy: clearer understanding of the workings of self-organizing clusters among innovative firms and industrial regions in Northern Italy, Germany and Scandinavia may well provide a basis for more effective restructuring strategies in declining industrial areas, and better timescales and learning strategies for the many efforts now under way to incubate newer industries.
- Knowledge-sharing networks: strategies for 'disseminating' good practice, whether on companies' social performance, educational innovation or cross-sector partnership, may need more active participation by network members than conventional approaches to information-sharing allow.
- New regulatory models: one goal of new regulatory frameworks for business might be to encourage 'self-governance' in social and environmental performance, requiring common minimum standards but also rewarding and seeking to amplify innovative problem-solving by firms.
- Learning by doing: public and governmental programmes aimed at encouraging behavioural change, whether by trade unions, companies, social sector organizations or universities should include an expectation of high failure rates as a condition of long-term success, and seek to structure funding streams so that they follow effective learning over time rather than encourage inflexibility.

CONCLUSION

The search for a successful European enterprise model may not lie in looking for the ideal balance between market and state, regulation and commercial freedom, but by seeking to understand the characteristics of complex systems that can adapt purposefully over time to drastic changes in their operating environment, and then building governance structures that reflect these principles. The purpose needs to be driven by the desire to meet more complex, diverse forms of human need in a less predictable environment.

This process of institutional change, given that it will involve high levels of institutional failure and disruption, needs the active consent of citizens. Systems of governance that distribute the responsibility for innovation and responsiveness more widely will depend more heavily on the active contribution of citizens, whether at work or at large in their communities. In this sense, the struggle to synthesize entrepreneurship into a systematic process of institutional change is also part of the effort to reinvent democracy itself.

Transmodern Dialogues Of Society

A role for business

Marc Luyckx, Vision 2020

11 SEPTEMBER 2001: ENTERING A PARADIGM SHIFT?

The crime that was perpetrated against innocent US citizens on 11 September 2001 could be interpreted as a signal that humanity is entering into a grey circle of danger at the crossroads of four curves. In history, whenever humanity has been confronted with such important paradigm shifts, it has always been a period of political turbulence, wars and violence. Almost all the governments in the world have rightly condemned this act of extreme violence. However, it could also show that the values propagated by the West are no longer accepted as self-evident in many countries, and even in the European Union (EU) and the US itself. It could be a signal of the paradigm shift, beyond modernity and towards transmodernity.

In the diagram opposite the short bold line above 11 September 2001 indicates a possible short circuit which the business avant-garde could help the political class to use, in order to avoid violence and war. They could help politicians to understand concretely the new logic, which I call the transmodern one. And they could also show politicians how to realize the transition.

DEFINITION OF THREE PARADIGMS

A paradigm is a complicated word to indicate the implicit values of a

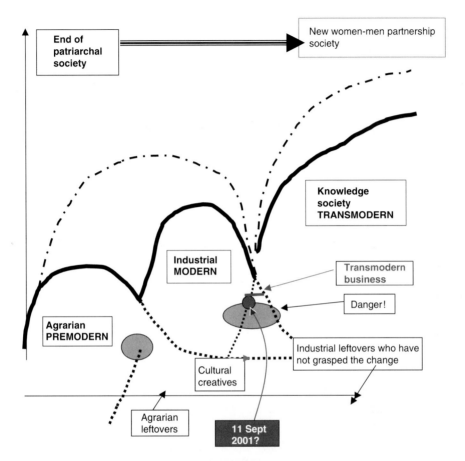

THE END OF MODERNITY, PATRIARCHALISM AND CAPITALISM

civilization. It is like the invisible set of basic values which are never discussed because they are self-evident to all political parties and all of civil society. At times like the Renaissance, or even the Reformation, there has been a shift in those basic societal assumptions. And there has been a conflict between the premodern and modern paradigms which has led to long religious war.

History shows us indeed that differences between basic values can lead to very violent wars, where the reason for the war is not even evident, but aggression is present because the 'other's' system is a death threat to our own system of basic values.

Let us now analyze three different paradigms: the premodern, the modern and the transmodern.

THE PREMODERN PARADIGM

1. This paradigm is vertical and authoritarian. Authority comes from the top, from God Himself, who transmits this truth directly to the clergy, who are allowed to teach governments and the faithful, men and then finally women.

2. This paradigm is patriarchal: God Himself is the warrant of this order where man dominates woman and is the only bearer of the sacred word. Women are supposed to stay at home to nurture their children and provide their children's education. If a woman dares to oppose this order, for example in asking to become part of the clergy, she is immediately in danger of being considered to have been corrupted by the forces of darkness and of being seen as a witch and burned at the stake.

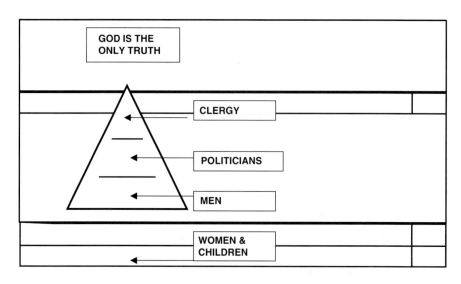

THE PREMODERN PARADIGM

3. Premodernity is intolerant. Its Truth is exclusive. It is only our religion and no one else's that owns the Truth. This Truth has been trusted to us by God Himself. It is thus impossible and impious to even think that another Truth could exist. Holy wars, crusades and inquisition are normal consequences of this concept of Truth.

4. Premodernity is opposed to secularization. The very concept of secularization is considered as a blasphemy. Atheists are tolerated when it is no longer possible to kill them.

5. This symbolic system has the great advantage of being stable and poetic. Everything has a deep and eternal meaning that is decided by God in eternity. There is no values crisis. The young generation has no difficulty in reproducing the values of their parents, because they are sacred and stable. This system is built to last forever.

6. This system is enchanted. The Cosmos is reflecting God's glory. Everything is full of poetry and sacredness. Believers have a deep sense of the sacred.

7. The theological and political weight of the clergy is evident – at least in the western 'Religions of the Book'. They have an enormous hold on the souls and the bodies of the faithful. This can lead, and has led, to the worst religious and political abuses.

8. There is only one science: theology. Everybody spoke Latin in the universities of the Middle Ages. There was a real universality of thought and of language which would prevail for centuries.

9. Premodernity has a sense of the sacred, which is evident and not even disputed.

This paradigm is called 'fundamentalist' by some.

THE MODERN PARADIGM

1. Modernity is vertical and authoritarian in the public sphere. It has not suppressed the power pyramid of the Middle Ages. It has simply switched God with the Goddess 'Reason' . This means that what is not rational has no value anymore, at least in the public sphere.

2. Modernity is patriarchal. Despite what is said it continues to exclude

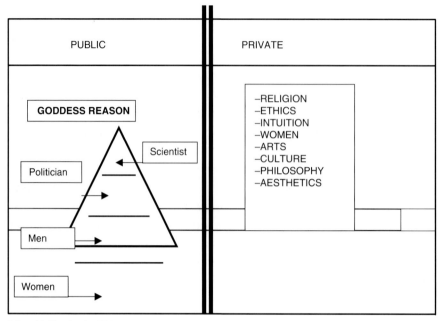

THE MODERN PARADIGM

    women. This time it is because they are 'less rational' and thus incapable of taking rational public decisions.

3. Modernity is intolerant. Its concept of Truth is exclusive: there is no Truth except rational Truth, at least in the public sphere. The non-rational approaches are simply *not* taken into consideration. Intolerance is systematic towards the non-western ways of thinking. This leads to new and more subtle forms of crusade, inquisition and holy war in the name of progress, development, structural adjustment etc.

4. Modernity has secularized the world (secular being what defines itself without reference to any God). Modernity has introduced a very useful distinction between religious and profane, but this distinction has become a strict separation. On one side you now have the serious, public, rational, masculine, economic and scientific pole which has the power. And on the other you have the intuitive, philosophical, religious, aesthetic and

feminine pole which has been relegated to the private with no political power at all. A wall of absolute separation has been built between the public and the private.

5. Modernity has switched the concept of stability with the one of progress. Progress is considered as a value in itself without discussion. The concept of stability has been lost and is even considered obsolete.

6. Max Weber was perfectly right: modernity has disenchanted the world. Our souls have no oxygen in this secular society. Apart from Goddess Reason, there is no stable basis for fundamental values. Every allusion to an inward and deep dimension of human existence is forbidden in public, except for at burials or on exceptional occasions. The world is only rational. Religions are expected to disappear slowly but forever. The only possible enchantment is provided by progress in science and technology.

7. Renaissance has used reason in order to be rid of the power and obscurantism of the clergy. This has been a liberation. But modernity has unconsciously reintroduced a new calling which is functioning exactly in the same way: the technocrats and the scientists. Their power is as important and undisputed. They are dictating orders to politicians and to the public at large. One famous example is the unchallenged power of the economists over the governments of the world.

8. In introducing new and sane distinctions, modernity has allowed the birth of science and technology, but also of all the other disciplines we use today like ethics, aesthetics, mathematics, physics, chemistry etc. Unfortunately, those distinctions have become strictly compart-mentalized, which forbids any real transdisciplinary creative work today. The global holistic view has been completely lost. Science analyzes every tree, every branch, every root etc, but is unable to see the forest.

9. In the public sphere modernity leaves absolutely no place for any form of the sacred. In this disenchanted world there is thus a crisis of fundamental values. Meanwhile science is reintroducing a kind of sacredness of rationality. If a reasoning is 'rational' it is acceptable everywhere and for every culture, at any time. But this very new sacred rationality is also in crisis today, simply because fewer people believe that science and technology are able, by themselves, to solve the huge

problems of today.

THE TRANSMODERN PARADIGM

1. Transmodernity is democratic. Everyone is on an equal footing around the same table in order to discuss together common problems, putting national interests aside. This is an ethical quantum leap.
2. Transmodernity is post-patriarchal. There is no no longer any reason to introduce any kind of discrimination. On the contrary, women's vision and intuition are indispensable in order to invent quickly innovative solutions.
3. Transmodernity is tolerant by definition. This tolerance is active. Its definition of the Truth is inclusive. All cultures and all citizens in the

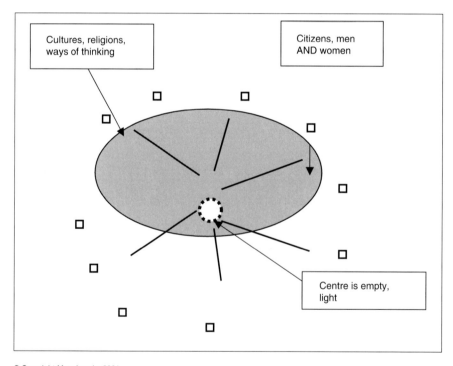

© Copyright Marc Luyckx 2001

THE TRANSMODERN PARADIGM

world are included. Everyone is encouraged to follow their own path towards the centre, towards wisdom and illumination.

4. Transmodernity establishes and redefines a new relation between religion and politics. On the one hand, one has to avoid any confusion between religion and politics, as in the Middle Ages, but on the other hand one has to abolish the modern separation which finally becomes a refusal of any spiritual dimension at all and produces disenchantment. Transmodernity is thus post-secular.

5. Beyond premodern stability and modern quantitative progress, transmodernity proposes the concept of transformation. The aim is a better personal and collective life for humanity and for the environment.

6. Transmodernity is able to re-enchant the world because it will reopen access to the soul. The spiritual dimension is not taboo anymore. It will help towards a new kind of reconciliation between our bodies and souls, and between our minds and our souls. This reconciliation will unleash an enormous amount of positive and creative energy which is the opposite of disenchantment. Re-enchantment begins when our souls begin to be liberated and begin to hope again. However, transmodernity could degenerate into a greater disenchantment if this transformation is not real and deep.

7. Transmodernity cancels and dissolves completely the very notion of clergy, technocrat or specialist. In every domain citizens want to have power over their own lives, and over their intimate relationships with the divine. The concept of a necessary intermediary between God and man becomes less accepted.

8. Transmodernity fundamentally redefines the relationship between science, ethics and society. Science itself is going through a deep transformation. It is decompartmentalizing the various scientific disciplines, and looking for real and radical transdisciplinarity. It tries to integrate ethics and meaning at all levels. The very distinction between hard and soft sciences becomes obsolete.

9. Transmodernity is trying to rediscover the sacred as a dimension of life, but in a non-vertical system of power and in an inclusive definition of the Truth.

A NEW KIND OF WAR AND TWO KINDS OF ENEMY

A NEW KIND OF WAR: A WAR BETWEEN (INVISIBLE) PARADIGMS

My hypothesis is that we are assisting today in a war between paradigms, between visions of the world, rather than a war between religions. It is important, even crucial, for the EU to understand this new type of war in order to invent and adapt a new strategy. The new strategy must, in my opinion, start with the careful analysis of the (new) nature of the conflict.

TWO KINDS OF ENEMY

There are two kinds of enemy. The classic enemy, who wants to take your money or your territory. Only a sane balance of violence is able to counter this invader. Most of our strategies are constructed to deal with this kind of enemy.

But there is also the religious martyr type of enemy. This is a fighter who, like the first Christians, has a spiritual motivation and has absolutely no fear of death. He is beyond fear. He knows why he is living and why he is dying. And the more we kill this type of enemy, the more we create.

The only strategy to counter this new kind of enemy is 'probity' or justice. And so we must ask ourselves, are we doing enough economically to help the majority of the world's population to escape from poverty? Are we really preparing a sustainable world for our children?

TRANSMODERNITY AS A NEW DIALOGUE

In the actual context of the attack on the US by terrorists, the majority of political observers agree that we are not witnessing a conflict of civilizations – although there are real dangers of conflict proliferation. And the main and most violent conflicts are between the premoderns and the moderns, inside each religion – usually the transmoderns are ignored.

Every religion has its 'fundamentalists'. The 'fundamentalists' are in fact premodern, and they are to be found in Christianity, Judaism and Islam. They all claim that 'modernity' has killed the soul of the people in negating the spiritual dimension of life, at least in public affairs. They also claim that, having no spiritual dimension, modernity has fostered materialism and egocentrism and killed generosity and solidarity. And they claim that the West is impoverishing them more and more. They are thus fighting against modernity. Are they completely wrong?

What are we saying then? Modern western governments claim that premoderns are intolerant and impose their views, and their 'divine' truth. But they also claim that everyone should accept human rights and modernization, and that there is no solution other than to join our system of free trade. Does this not mean that the West is equally intolerant?

When we listen to some of the declarations of the Bush administration, one sometimes has the impression that Max Weber's analysis is right. In the sense that US leaders claim that their economic success is a sign of God's blessing, they are in a way also premodern or 'fundamentalist'. One could have here, not a clash of civilizations, but a clash between two fundamentalisms. This can become very violent.

What will be the EU's position? Is there a way out? In my hypothesis the way forward is transmodernity, which is already being lived by 25% of US and EU citizens and perhaps also in other cultures. It is important to note that 66% of this new group are women.

It seems that an important part of Islam could be silently trying to become transmodern: keeping the best of modern discoveries, but rediscovering the lost dimensions of life – aesthetics, spirituality, feminine values of caring etc.

If this is the case, governments should stop characterizing as fundamentalist every movement rediscovering the lost dimensions of modernity. If this is true, European foreign policy should try to build bridges with all transmoderns – in all cultures – who are preparing the world civilization of tomorrow.

But this presupposes that one is willing to go beyond modernity, which seems to be very difficult for many.

A CRUCIAL ROLE FOR THE TRANSMODERN BUSINESS

According to my observation, there is a minority of business leaders around the world who are like an *'avant-garde'* movement. They have accepted fully the challenge of the knowledge society and of the new paradigm. They have understood from inside the actual transformation of the world. And they have not only understood the transformation, they have been successful in enacting it in their enterprise.[1] They are a very significant minority. They have a world political vocation: to help the political institutions to understand and cope with the change. They could be of crucial importance in helping the political class to look for new global strategies and policies. Their credibility is exceptional, precisely because of their concrete success in realizing the change in their enterprise and perhaps in themselves.

[1] For example, Dee Hock, the founder of VISA, Rinaldo Brutoco, founder with Willis Harman of the 'World Business Academy', and others like Verna Allee, Susan Mehrtens and many other women business leaders.
Hock, Dee, *The Chaordic Organization*, Berrett-Koehler, San Francisco, October 2000
Mehrtens, Susan, 'Learning designs and the Third Wave' in *Perspectives on Business and Global Change*, World Business Academy, Volume 13, Number 4, December 1999, p. 59
Allee, Verna, 'New tools for the new economy' in *Perspectives on Business and Global Change*, World Business Academy, Volume 13, Number 4, December 1999, p. 59

Evolution Management

Circumventing the Cartesian trap

Marc Van Der Erve, Evolution Management

THE CARTESIAN TRAP

'Encapsulating' ideas have been developed about the evolution of society and how we might influence its course towards a higher societal order. The tendency to classify our world and our urge to break it down into pieces (and to use these pieces as building blocks of models that we can manipulate and explain) has been the core of our way of thinking, roughly since the 16th century. The Frenchman, Descartes, who sought to shake off the mystique of medieval times, has become the most recognized proponent of this approach.

Indeed, Cartesian thinking or classification has since been ruling our scientific endeavours. The drift to digitalize our world has been a visible result. Indeed, classification or 'digitalization' has been immensely successful if we take into account our technological achievements so far. But, classification can also be an evil in disguise as it is the root of fascist thinking, ethnic cleansing and extremism often feeding the notion of 'I and we' and, thus, of 'we and they' to poor and bored minds that have often only religion to digest.

As recent shockwaves of terror have shown, the chances are slim that we are able to reframe the views of people just by holding up a mirror of societal development. Like the depressive patients of Carl Jung, only the possibility of a meaningful coincidence (or synchronicity) might generate a sense of solace and hope. However much it flirts with dynamics, the two-dimensional Cartesian world alone will never be able to rise above a sinuous, meandering path that passes restrictive and still stages for as far as we can see.

A Cartesian world view resembles the view of a child before puberty. The child and its parents may experience a remarkable harmony because the child has sorted out its environment, accepting its players and their roles. This peace and quiet, though, will soon depart as the child's hormones start disturbing the balance by changing its being inside out.

The anthropologist, Gregory Bateson, generally identified as the inventor of social cybernetics, warns us to back off when it comes to classification and to look at the *process*: 'Rather than to determine how two shells differ in shape, form etc, why not look at what (process) they have in common?'

THE THIRD DIMENSION

We have reached an era in which we have greatly enhanced our ability to create and identify *physical devices*, such as networks and computers, as well as *social devices*, such as values, rules and organizations both spontaneous and deliberate. In fact, through social devices, we organize and create meaning.

Nowadays, the complexity is such that even the constructs of our own making become too difficult to predict and manage. Just look at the stock market! Much like our brains, our constructs start behaving as 'operationally closed' systems that, although they can be influenced from outside, are mainly driven by their internal complexity.

The discovery of self-organizing behaviour in biological systems first and social systems later, by Varela and Maturana, may have been coincidental, but it has certainly been timely. Self-organizing behaviour serves as an explanation of these complexities not by classification but by describing dynamic aspects of continuous interaction. Two fundamental qualities of, if not conditions for, self-organizing behaviour are autonomy and complexity. In other words, only autonomous and complex systems might develop self-organizing behaviour. So, in my publication *Evolution*

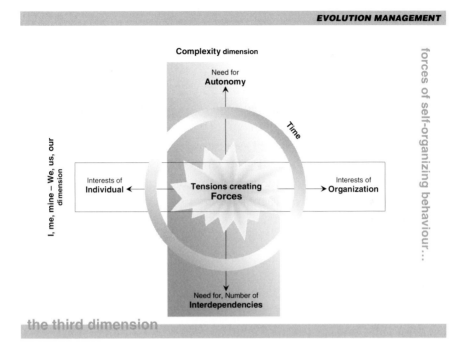

Management, self-organizing behaviour helped me to identify the third dimension, in fact, one that is representing the tension field between *the need for autonomy and the need for interdependency*. This third dimension, I suggest, should be identified as the *complexity dimension*.

To obtain a scalable and quantifiable form for the complexity dimension, I chose to represent complexity as 'the number of interdependencies' within an organization or society (after all, the number of interdependencies increases and decreases as organizations and societies evolve).

In this way, I obtained three dimensions. *Time*, as the 'force of history', is the *first* dimension. The tension between individual, organizational and societal needs, the so-called *I and we dimension*, is the *second* dimension. The *complexity dimension* is the *third* dimension. The second and third dimensions together will indeed show a spiraling trace along the axis of time.

However, with self-organizing systems comes their by-product: the human brain might produce compositions, organizations might generate revenue and societies might produce Nobel prize winners. Of course, other relevant examples can be identified for each and every self-organizing social system. In effect, the path in time that an organization or society follows coincides with the rate of natural growth of their produce. In other words, time can be represented by subsequent growth curves each of which reveals specific developmental challenges as well as prospects.

At first sight, this might seem too far fetched. But if you take the trouble to read the explanatory comments of Alan Greenspan in Senate hearings, you will discover how Greenspan articulates his insight by evaluating the impact of these natural growth curves on society.

Effectively, what value does the third dimension add to our understanding and interpretation of societal and organizational evolution?

First, the third dimension of complexity helps us make sense of 'order'

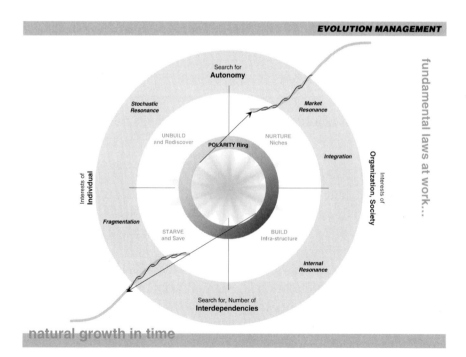

by expressing it in terms of an increasing or, for that matter, decreasing number of interdependencies. By decoupling 'societal order' from hierarchical value judgements, an objective instrument is created (effectively the 'platform of self-organizing behaviour') which will be more acceptable as a measuring stick in the eyes of the society or organization in question.

Second, the four quadrants bring fundamental processes together in distinct ways. Each quadrant evaluates the natural drift between individual and organizational interests as well as the rise and decline both of complexity and natural growth. Quadrants serve as cradles for the evaluation of fundamental processes in society, such as chaos, recombination, resonance, evolution, integration and fragmentation. By making the interaction more transparent, the third dimension invites the identification of organizational measures and the assessment of leadership styles. The latter is now being used regularly and with remarkable precision in executive search.

Third, strategic and leadership decisions that are made on the crossroads of these fundamental processes tend to be directional in nature. They leave room for societies and organizations to develop new values and rules, unprecedented 'social devices', when they recombine and select those that generate success under specific circumstances. Eventually, this dynamic perspective will be adopted when organizations and societies are forced to exchange eternal solutions with those that focus more effectively on situational and developmental circumstances.

Fourth, the dimension of complexity diminishes the degree of polarization as it replaces classification-based judgemental stages of development with the fundamental notion of polarity. Polarity, because it is directional in nature, tends to amplify the needs of organizations and societies. It does not rub in certain predefined hierarchical ideas. As an instrument, the polarity ring connects the four opposite poles on the platform of self-organizing behaviour.

In a dynamic world-view, polarity is crucial because it helps us interpret and identify forces between people, societies and organizations that attract at one point in time and repel at another. The approach of Alcoholics

Anonymous, for example, makes use of this force when it brings together people who share the same problem. The search for a new sense of autonomy without alcohol fosters togetherness. As such, this force develops to draw people together. Similarly, on the internet, certain websites bring together people who share a tragic loss or a terrible disease. In search of solace, website visitors seem to come from nowhere attracted by a common search for autonomy, spontaneously creating interdependencies on their way.

In enterprise, costly mistakes can be prevented when it comes to finding leadership, suppliers, alliance partners, mergers and acquisitions. Based on the developmental polarity of a company, new employees, suppliers and alliance partners can now be selected with a remarkable chance of success. Connections between societies may be contemplated, whatever their level of complexity, for as long as they share the same polarity. In other words, collaboration does not necessarily depend on the level of complexity or hierarchical order but on developmental polarity.

But, the force that attracts may also repel. When organizations or societies achieve an ultimate sense of either autonomy or interdependence, they will repel one another. For example, societies or organizations with too strong a sense of autonomy may collide as they are less capable of opening up to a societal perspective that is alien to them. The same applies to organizations and societies that develop an excessive focus on interdependencies. The latter generates 'we-versus-they' feelings. Generally, such behaviour turns out to be a prelude to an imminent breakup as such societies become less able to respond effectively to change.

Indeed, the complexity of our own creations demands that we focus on the primary forces of self-organizing behaviour. So, when it comes to elaborations on evolution and development, our understanding of forces and their behavioural impact can make a difference.

This observation seems timely as yet another flow of events is shaking the very ground on which we stand.

SUPERSTRING SOCIETY

An increasingly dense telecommunication network is being spun around the world. And the number of interactions that it sustains multiplies exponentially as not just individuals and computers are connected but networks of networks of networks. As a result, 'strings' of actions and reactions are generated across a broad spectrum of society. These actions and reactions travel like waves, triggering other strings each capable of shattering established institutions and ideas. For those who think that the internet is being regulated and brought under control, just wait and see what happens when internet-phones reach their potential, both numerically and application-wise.

Traditionally, organizations and societies seek to create a framework of rules, conventions, laws, rituals and values allowing them to execute efficiently their primary tasks. And for those societies and organizations whose tasks do not change, this still applies. But in enterprise which increasingly revolves around the creation of virtual knowledge-driven products, the very framework that promised protection now creates stagnation. Banks in particular are facing this dilemma. The competitive barriers, which they erected in the form of rules, attitudes, systems and networks of branches, are now boxing them in. Not hindered by historical heritage, affinity banking experiments by others will use the internet to reach out to multiple and precise selections of clients. They will do so extremely efficiently using collaborative business models. But, what is more important, they will have the capacity to adapt constantly to evolving client needs as well as social trends.

In a 'networked society', the need to adapt rises in step with an exponential increase in activity. Achieving competitive advantage by focusing on just one competitor simply becomes a waste of time. Competitive skirmishes are not productive in a networked society. Winning one combat means leaving many competitors unvanquished. An entirely new challenge emerges in the form of 'multitude' (of interactions). Making grandiose and even more complex models does not make sense. A multitude of interactions will force us to revise these models constantly as new variations of trends, findings, values and ideas develop. In a networked society, multitude indeed adds *quantum-like* qualities to behaviour.

Physics offers a tempting analogy, which deals with the unification of

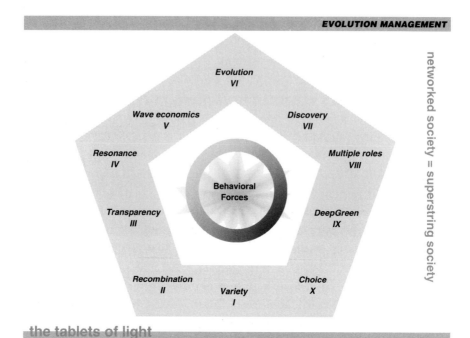

forces. The 'theory of strings' tries to explain the forces in nature by one and the same *dynamic* phenomenon in the form of a 'string'. A string is a minute device representing force. Each string has an infinite number of vibration modes, which make it behave like the string of a musical instrument. The frequency with which a string vibrates effectively determines its role. In my publication *Tablets of Light*, I explore ten qualities of resonating forces in the networked society which, in certain respects, parallel the ten qualities (or dimensions) of 'strings' in nature. These qualities or behavioural laws are rooted in dynamic phenomena.

The following is a summary of ten fundamental laws that determine the behavioural forces in a 'networked society'. Each law leads to the next.

I – *VARIETY*, NOT VICTORY, IS THE TRUE SOURCE OF COMPETITION

As I mentioned before, the traditional idea of competition does not hold in a world of multiple interactions. Competition becomes less of a one-to-one battle and more of a competition between species. Responsiveness (to changing environmental situations) is what results in survival. Variety (of species, ideas, products and organizations) betters the chance of meeting the needs of the environment. Societies and organizations can create variety by division or specialization, a principle that Adam Smith recognized. However, collaborative business models are needed in order to ensure that each division contributes to the responsiveness of the whole.

II – *RECOMBINATION* IS THE PLATFORM OF PROGRESS

When variety has been achieved through division, this law ensures that the produce of each division can be recombined. We share our ability to combine diverse, at-first-sight unrelated, matters only with our genes. Re-combinations comprise physical and social devices. Social devices have a virtual make-up and play a role in the organization both of physical and social devices. Social devices, such as language, stories, values, rules, processes and organizations, also give meaning. We need connectivity (and connectivity needs protocols) to foster and achieve recombination.

III – *TRANSPARENCY* IS AT THE HEART OF WEALTH DISTRIBUTION

Transparency is an essential quality which ensures that recombination (of ideas, for example) takes place. The market mechanism of supply and demand describes one form of recombination. In the networked society, websites are junctions where supply meets demand; they are essential instruments that ensure transparency. Transparency helps in 'wealth' distribution by providing insight into the unfolding market mechanism. Not 'big brother' but recombination and the market mechanism are at stake.

IV – *RESONANCE* IS THE ULTIMATE SIGNAL OF OPPORTUNITY

Resonance refers to a down-to-earth principle in physics which involves forces. Also in society, internal forces may build up to a point where established combinations are shattered and new combinations emerge. Several events needed to resonate before the stone axe came about. Its emergence required the increasing brain complexity of early humans, their changing way of life when turning from scavengers to hunters, the resulting demand for wooden hunting tools, the need for more robust woodworking devices, the availability of the right material and the mobility of early humans (to spread the technology) when moving with the animals they hunted. Resonance requires (a certain number of) interdependencies, ie complexity, in a society or organization.

V – *WAVE ECONOMICS* ARE AT THE CORE OF COMMITMENT AND REWARD

When resonance occurs, wave economics determine the commitment of resources that trigger and foster natural growth. Natural growth follows a distinct pattern, which allows us to refine the timing of our efforts and investment. The rate of natural growth also helps us identify the appropriate management style.

VI – *EVOLUTION* IS THE PATH TO SUPREME FUNCTIONALITY

Evolution is about natural selection in a certain environment. The environment is generally so complex that it is impossible to determine what exactly caused natural selection or resonance. By simplifying the environment, we can make the process of natural selection work for us. Several generations of species may help us achieve remarkable functionality both for physical and social devices.

VII – *DISCOVERY* IS THE ORIGIN OF LEARNING

In an environment of multitude that is in constant flux, our method of learning will change. As animal experiments have shown, exploration leaves an instant and distinct trace in the brain. It appears to be a most efficient and inspiring way of learning. Today's learning systems present us with models that have been explored by others. Confronted with the internet as a repository of knowledge, repetition (our traditional way of learning) becomes inefficient. The models that we internalize by repetition become mental anchors that discourage further exploration. More than repetition, exploration fosters intuition. On its path of trial and error, while searching for direction, exploration challenges our reason and grows our sense of 'knowing'. Exploration is the precondition of discovery and learning in an environment of multitude. In our explorations, we will discover tempting environments. Where and who do we want to be?

VIII – MULTIPLE, ALBEIT VIRTUAL, ROLES ARE THE GATEWAYS TO FREEDOM

Roles have an empowering impact, even if they are not real. Not specialization but ambition, the capacity to stir the environment and chance determine our role in society. Medieval society recognized only three roles: those who pray, those who fight and those who work. Other roles (of merchants for example) were simply ignored. Some of today's societies are not so different from medieval ones in that they also deny the roles of their people. The networked society, with its capacity to connect, invites the creation of new dimensions of freedom, new societies and communities. In fact, connectivity enables people (even the suppressed) to assume a variety of roles. The ability to assume multiple roles in various environments fosters recombination and improves the chance of achieving resonance. Roles also create order, which conditions organizations or societies to achieve common goals. Multiple roles require connectivity and communication.

IX– DEEPGREEN (TAKING DISTANCE) YIELDS CULTURAL AND SOCIAL FERTILITY

Soil that is contaminated is cleaned through so-called thermal desorption. Essentially, by heating contaminated soil, the pollutants escape in gas form. The soil comes out clean and fertile. The development of societies and organizations also produces residues that may intoxicate 'the soil' on which growth emerges. Arnold Toynbee observes how civilizations initially grow and then decline when they are no longer able to respond successfully to challenges. The networked society brings matters of growth and decline to a different level. By connecting players from societies and organizations around the world, it will arouse a self-awareness which relates challenges to those of others. Indeed, in search of growth, self-awareness may heat the soil that makes polluting rules escape. These rules will not be lost forever: as common historical sediment, they will be absorbed by the network; as pollutants to one, rules may become food for recombination by others.

Distancing oneself from the warm embrace of restraining rules and roles requires solace through connection. But, how do we find constancy in greater variety?

X – *CHOICE* IS AT THE CENTRE OF STABILITY AND TOGETHERNESS

We have come full circle and arrived at the important notion of variety again. How do we encourage variety? Indeed, having a choice requires variety. On the other hand, the multitude of alternatives that we will have access to in the networked society will affect us most. Having a choice leads to economic benefits but it may also have a destabilizing effect on our life. Choice may tease us to the extent that it fosters feelings of missing out on certain opportunities. In the networked society, stability comes when making choices, even less astute ones. Interestingly, the reticular system of the brain will try to justify our choice by (subconsciously) identifying others who have come to the same conclusion. Hence, whether it concerns cars, partners or religion, choice actually brings us together as a 'flocking device'.

In summary, the above behavioural laws guide us in plucking the strings of resonating forces in order to generate novel devices both physical and social. The ten behavioural laws of the networked society are 'social devices' that are rooted in a non-judgemental, dynamic world-view which fosters *plurality*. After all, plurality is a precondition of survival.

COMPLEXITY, PURPOSE AND BELIEF

In practical terms, the future world of enterprise will be paradoxical. On the one hand, our awareness of our options will be increasing dramatically while, on the other hand, we will find ourselves and our companies being part of a natural, non-linear drift which is more difficult to control.

As elements of a more interactive and complex environment, managers will find it more difficult to distance themselves so as to observe the full evolutionary spectrum of their organization (observer's dilemma). Hence, a new kind of consulting is likely to emerge. So-called evolution management (EM) consultants will help make sense of the pertinent dynamic parameters that are at stake when organizations develop, no matter what the context. EM consultants should suggest areas of expertise and external relationships that might need to be brought into the process in order to regain organizational responsiveness and, thus, developmental potential. On the other hand, EM consultants should help managers relate their companies and organizations to the quantum-like dynamics of the networked society.

Interestingly, the efforts to demystify societal and cultural evolution have added another problem. By defining the timeless parameters of societal development, we actually let in through the back door the mystique of non-linearity that comes with complexity. As a result, another perspective may be needed to preserve our sense of purpose. Indeed, on the edge of chaos and order, only religion or faith can do so. Unfortunately, to a greater or lesser extent, current-day religions tend to be contextual if you take into account the rules (of the past) with which they confine their followers. It may not be a new messiah but a new religion that is required.

Humanism And Enterprise

Bo Ekman, Nextwork

'Humanism is a democratic and ethical life stance, which affirms that human beings have the right and responsibility to give meaning and shape to their own lives. It stands for the building of a more humane society through ethics based on human and other natural values in a spirit of reason and free inquiry through human capabilities. Humanism is not by definition theistic and does not accept supra-natural views of reality.'

The International Humanistic and Ethical Union in 1996 offered this definition of humanism. It strongly underwrites a vision of a democratic organization of society where we, as individuals, have rights and responsibilities. But the humanistic vision of society understands that human beings are an integrated part of nature. What is human is natural. The humanistic vision of humanity includes the human capacity for wisdom, reason and expansion of human capabilities. The humanistic vision is dynamic, not static; it is systemic, not linear. It is thus in conflict with the dominating world-view of the industrial (mechanistic) paradigm: linear, hierarchical, predictable, collectivist.

To be humanistic means to many – not least in the world of business – to be soft, to be do-gooders dealing with philosophy for philosophy's sake. They are expected to put on kid gloves when dealing with serious situations. Humanistic is *not* a prefix usually used to portray strong leadership. Strong leaders are primarily expected to deal with substance rather than principles, people and relations. Therefore, we have a leadership culture where we encourage results rather than purpose, power rather than principles, style rather than context, growth rather than development and, indeed, management rather than leadership. Visit the management section in any bookshop and see how full they are of 'How-To' and '10-Steps-To' books. The psychology shelf is no better, and as a result organizations and businesses are ridden more by fear than by trust.

I work with the conviction that human development must precede economic growth. Economic growth provides means for further human development. Humanistic leadership is not exploitative in its intent. Its intent is to improve the quality and quantity of human, social, natural and financial capital in the process of satisfying new levels of human needs. This is an evolutionary process, seldom in harmony; always in change. The economy and the capitalist process is as natural as nature itself; in fact it is a niche of nature.

Thus, humanistic leadership must be based on an understanding of the whole, not just of technology or economics, or shareholder value *per se*. Humanistic leadership is based on an understanding of the governing principles of the interacting systems of production, nature, society, ecology and the market. Humanistic leadership is a process of widening one's worldview, wisdom and understanding; it is a process of development, of evolution. We need tough results-orientated humanistic leaders who can reconcile principles and results.

BP's vision is to take the company beyond petroleum. Ikea's vision is to provide quality furniture for the common people. Swedbank's vision is to provide the destitute with professional banking services and make money in the process. This is humanistic leadership. Humanistic leadership stems from a passion for principles and love for people. The opposite – cynicism, bad principles and contempt for people – corrupt the exercise of power. It took a tough result-orientated humanist to bring independence to India, freedom to South Africa and civil rights to America. These guys were no sissies. We need that kind of leadership for the resolution of global warming, the quality of education, the jamming of our roads, the provision of water and the resolution of conflict.

The world of business, for its own self-interest, should I believe adopt a vision of bringing another three billion people into the dynamics of the market economy over the next 25 years. That's principled pragmatic business for you. In 1900, less than 10% of the world's population were actors in the market economy. In 1950 we were up to 25% – 400 to 500 million were actors in the internationalized economy. And today we have reached three billion – 50%. This growth of 2.5 billion has been the backbone to economic growth. Human development precedes economic growth.

Now, let's adopt the vision: we could expand the market economy with *another* three billion, but it will take a focused strategy of human development. This can happen, provided that we can adopt four sets of shared values and principles for local and global governance. The first relates to democracy, the second to human rights and the third to sustainability. The fourth set refers to the principles of the market economy.

Humanistic leadership has always been around. But I use the concept as an antithesis to the kind of leadership that has dominated over the last 15 years – an ultra-economistic leadership in the pursuit of shareholder value. The shareholder value model rests on a brutal simplification of reality. We have experienced unprecedented economic growth through the 1990s, coupled with astronomical growth of Profit to Equity ratios and stock values around the globe. This development was released by a combination of Thatcherism/Reaganism and the advent of an avalanche of new technologies. The new technologies, and in particular the breakthrough of the Web in the 1990s, triggered globalization.

The combination of new technologies and shareholder value capitalism gave birth to the short era of the 'new economy'. Those were the days. Thomas Friedman named the actors of the global financial community the 'electronic herd' and found, in his book *The Lexus and the Olive Tree*, that businesses deterministically were caught by the 'golden straightjacket' – perform or die. The technology is here to stay but the expectations on its sudden wealth-creating magic are gone.

This kind of neo-liberal capitalism, or *laissez-faire* capitalism, set off prairie fires of privatization, deregulation and trade liberation. These dynamics did, in fact, out-compete both the post-war European welfare state type of mixed economy capitalism and the communistic model of state capitalism. Both these political systems had, however, integrated social values and considerations into their moderation of *laissez-faire* capitalism of the period up to the Great Depression.

With the success of shareholder value/*laissez-faire* capitalism the market also came to be expected to care for and solve the problems that governments previously were supposed to take care of: solidarity, care for the elderly, education, equality and legal institutions. The support of these needs has gradually decreased. Social safety nets are less dependable.

Today, *laissez-faire* globalization has come under serious attack. In the wake of the growing problems of the environment, of the poor, of inequalities and health, literally hundreds of thousands of non-governmental organizations (NGOs) have started to formulate new political platforms. They seem to take over where the welfare state or the socialist states left off. These movements converged in Seattle, Washington, Prague, Gothenburg, Genoa and Barcelona. They converge on the Net. The image of the self-absorbed, isolated leaders in Genoa while 120,000 people workshopped and demonstrated is powerful. I doubt that a Gandhi or a Martin Luther King would not have reached out, walked the streets and asked, 'Tell me, what are your concerns?'

We have a new consciousness among consumers concerning child labour, human rights and the environment. If Ikea or Nike or Shell are found with their fingers in the pot we are going after them. A new climate is emerging. We are moving into the *post-new economy* where business and governments are being forced to reconcile the pursuit of results with principles. Does anyone think that the present organization of markets can win by battling down the protests? Or, should police shoot bewildered demonstrators? You simply don't shoot screaming puberty. And that's where the debate on globalization is; it is at the screaming puberty stage.

Most of these groups (and I talk to some of them) are simply asking business to become more democratic, asking business leaders to be more true to their principles – to the principles they apply to their own children – that freedom is not only for the global elite in their modern version of the Deer Park. Davos – where this elite meets within barbed wire – can stand as a symbol for the corporate and political elites to maintain the *status quo* of their power positions in a *laissez-faire* state of affairs.

We badly need new institutions that earn their legitimacy out of bottom-up democratic processes and accountability. We need:

1. New global institutions with executive powers that can oversee the most rapid possible globalization of *democracy* and the rule of law.
2. The fastest penetration of *human rights.*
3. Authorities that can manage global *environmental threats.*
4. Regional and global authorities in defence of *competition* and the *free market.*

The Hague Tribunal is a good start. These four principles must override and supersede the sovereignty of the nation state and certainly any single global corporation. This I see as a necessary step down the road to realize the vision of bringing another three billion people into the market economy. Thus there should not be any strategic or systematic conflict between democracy, human rights, ecology and the pursuit of economic growth that in the end will yield higher shareholder value.

SECTION 3

Globalization, Government And Europe

'The important thing for Government is not to do things which individuals are doing already, and to do them a little better or a little worse; but to do those things which at present are not done at all.'

The End of Laissez Faire Pt 4, John Maynard Keynes, 1926

The Challenges For Governments

Geoff Mulgan, the Cabinet Office

A hundred years ago, national governments and economies were generally ranked according to how large a military capacity they could sustain and how much territory they could govern. During the 20th century, by contrast, most came to be judged by the size of their GDP, or GDP per capita. During the last few years the focus has changed again, and economies are coming to be assessed in a more rounded way – taking into account people's quality of life and development, the state of the environment, human rights and how fairly life chances are distributed. There are three main reasons for this shift.

One concerns the past: an understanding that the success of economies has always rested on much more than free markets – just as important have been effective systems of health and learning, the rule of law and, crucially, how fairly and legimately rewards and opportunities are distributed.

A second concerns the present: the fact that people in their capacities as citizens, customers and shareholders increasingly look to public and private institutions to provide a balanced set of outputs.

A third concerns the future: a growing sense of our responsibility to leave behind a better legacy than we inherit – an improved environment, a greater stock of knowledge, higher values and stable institutions that are built to last.

European countries are each, in their different ways, evolving a new economic and social model which takes account of this more rounded view of the place of the economy. If there is one common feature of emerging approaches, it is that they are more systemic – seeing the links between education and health and the economy, between manufacturing and the environment, between domestic issues and global ones, and between actions and effects.

Every country has to fit new policies into its own political, cultural and institutional traditions but there are many overlapping themes. I want briefly to describe some of the new approaches being taken in the UK, as the government here attempts to achieve the triple goals of social cohesion, a high performance economy and a sustainable environment.

SOCIAL EXCLUSION AND POVERTY

The first priority has been to reverse the growth of poverty. Like many western countries, the UK experienced a significant worsening of social exclusion in the 1980s and early 1990s. A large minority was effectively cut out of the economy, with neighbourhoods run down and millions brought up in poverty and unemployment. Turning this around has required radical measures: a refashioned welfare system based on rights and responsibilities, support and pressure; holistic methods to tackle the needs of poor neighbourhoods in the round, covering everything from crime and health to transport and housing; much greater investment in early childhood, which we know has a huge pay-off later on; experimenting with new supports for social investment and enterprises; new ways of alleviating poverty, in particular through tax credits; and a much more concerted approach to engaging business and the voluntary sector as partners. This will undoubtedly be a long process, but major advances have already been made, including a 75% reduction in long-term youth unemployment. And long-term, no economy that fails to provide opportunities for large proportions of the population can expect to remain legitimate.

WORKFORCE DEVELOPMENT

The second priority has been upward mobility. The nations of the West have a far worse record on social mobility than they often claim. Yet continuous development of people's skills and continual chances to progress is not just important socially, it also lies at the heart of the new economy, and applies not just in high-tech manufacturing but also in face to face services. For the UK a priority has been action to tackle a relatively poor record on literacy and numeracy, and poor schools. For people in work we are focusing attention on developing individuals – particularly those without basic skills – and integrating workforce development much more closely with business development, building on successful models like Investors in People. That will also include ensuring that many more skills are properly recognized and rewarded. Some of the tools are likely to include: Individual Learning Accounts for employees; careers advice at every age; stronger networks to support businesses; and a radical expansion of e-learning.

KNOWLEDGE

The third priority is investment in knowledge. Economists now estimate that at least 50% of growth comes from knowledge and its application. But governments are only slowly moving from rhetoric to policy. A higher proportion of the UK population graduates than any other in Europe, but we are keen to raise this figure even higher, to around 50%. Beyond that the key strategies for knowledge include: substantially greater investment in basic science (and new ways of regulating the ethics of science in fields such as stem cell research); developing *milieux* in which innovation can thrive, often in big cities and linked to universities, with active venture capital industries; and, just as important, an emphasis on the crucial social and policy innovations that are as essential as new technologies and new science (supported, for example, through experimental zones for policy in schooling or health).

RESOURCE PRODUCTIVITY

The fourth priority has been a new approach to the environment. There has long been an unhealthy separation between environment and economy, and between environmental policy and economic policy. The UK recognizes that resource productivity needs to form a key part of any 21st century economic strategy. Making more from less, reducing waste, reducing inputs and achieving more closed systems of production and consumption offers a double dividend to business and society. However, it requires radical new approaches to renewable energy, recycling and the management of waste.

PUBLIC SERVICES

The fifth priority is the modernization of public services. During the 1970s and 1980s it was sometimes common to present public services as unproductive drains on the economy. This view was always misleading. Public services produce value as much as businesses do, and are an essential part of the productive system. When they are cut, the costs all too often show up in the form of high crime, insecurity, poor human development and ill-health. However, because they lack the pressures of the market, public services are often weak on innovation. Too often in the past large bureaucracies organized around 'command and control' principles took insufficient notice of the real concerns and needs of their users. We believe that the key task for reformers now is to redesign services much more clearly around the needs of users. That involves: providing much clearer entitlements of service, defined at national level; greater information and choice; more scope for innovation and entrepreneurialism; greater rewards and flexibility for staff; and more 'joining up' of different services to meet people's needs (for example e-services fitted around life transitions). In some fields that will involve radical use of technology; in others new kinds of partnerships with the private and voluntary sectors.

THE GLOBAL CONTEXT

In all of these areas we need a new approach to the boundaries between domestic policy and international policy. Government today takes place in a radically different environment from the past. Most areas of domestic policy are now also international – policing, migration, employment, technology. Today even the smallest organizations can achieve a global reach – whether for good or ill – and crises from the other side of the world soon affect us.

This new pattern of connectedness and interdependence requires a radical change in how governments and businesses operate. Shared responsibility is no longer optional. New forms of shared governance are now vital if we are to maximize the potential, and minimize the risks, of a much more connected world.

In the past Europe has often shown itself able to change rapidly. One virtue of being an old continent is that you know that change is essential to holding on to the things you value, let alone for creating new things. The fact that Europe now contains most of the nations that set the bench-mark world-wide in everything from productivity to health and environmental standards to social services is in part a result of past willingness to change and adapt – and a refusal to abide by the stereotype of a sclerotic, backward-looking region.

As a result of that past innovation we enter the new century in very propitious circumstances – if we fail to develop, test out and apply new models that can marry peace, prosperity and the needs of future generations we will have no one to blame but ourselves.

Geoff Mulgan writes in a personal capacity

8

The New Economy – Opportunity Or Threat?

Diane Coyle, Enlightenment Economics

The global downturn, in the wake of the burst dot.com bubble and the outbreak of a 'war against terrorism', cheered up some commentators enormously. These are the sceptics about the existence of anything that could be remotely described as a 'new economy'. After all, the return of hard times after the extraordinary 10-year US economic boom makes it more plausible to argue that nothing has really changed, that developments in the economy and society will continue to unfold in the ways they always have – and therefore that there is no particularly new challenge in devising policy responses to long-standing problems like unemployment, poverty, inequality, environmental degradation, regional imbalance and so on.

If only this were true, and none of us had to bother shedding our comfortable old views. Understanding and reacting to new situations is much harder work, after all.

Unfortunately, a difficult and important task lies ahead of anybody who wants to see a fairer and more prosperous Europe in future. For the caricature version of the new economy, the endless boom, soaring share prices and high-tech growth, was always a false portrait, and it's no surprise that it has faded so quickly. Rather, the phrase should be understood as a shorthand for fundamental structural changes in the leading market economies, changes driven largely by technology but also by other forces such as demographic change.

This new capitalism has been evolving slowly for many years, and aspects of it are so familiar we hardly bother to think about them any more. Among the most significant new economy trends are:

- The shift from manufacturing to services, meaning value added is based increasingly on interactions between people, not between man, material and machine.
- Changes in working patterns that vary by country depending on institutional arrangements and cultural preferences, but include part-time working, short-term contracts, shorter job tenure for many categories of employee, early retirement of older men and increased female participation in the workforce.
- Shorter median company lives, and a shift in typical company size towards the very small or the very large.
- Large-scale corporate restructuring since the early 1990s, including a huge merger wave, delayering of corporate hierarchies and massive cross-border investments.

It would take the most determined sceptic to deny the reality of these trends, which in their different ways reflect the plummeting cost of processing and transferring information and the increased importance of skills that complement the processing of information rather than of physical materials.

However, one element in the desire in some quarters to deny the reality of the new economy is the view that it inevitably involves a dog-eat-dog version of capitalism, giving priority to market forces, flexibility and other undesirable 'Anglo-Saxon' characteristics. From the progressive end of the political spectrum, enthusiasm for information technology and other aspects of high-tech has seemed intertwined with an eagerness to extend the scope of free markets and limit government intervention in the economy. Progressives fear the economic trends could force all of us into the same mould as the United States, with high rates of poverty and a high degree of inequality alongside high productivity and tremendous wealth creation.

Unfortunately, the ostrich position has already cost some European economies dear. Perhaps the most obvious price has been the persistence of high levels of unemployment in some countries, due in part to the resistance of political progressives to labour market reforms that are judged to be tainted with 'Anglo-Saxon' traits. But there are other costs too. Recent academic research has confirmed the instinct that a lack of 'flexibility' (specifically, a high degree of employment protection) in some Continental European countries has contributed significantly to the slower pace at which they have seen service sector industries increase their share in GDP and the fact that they have brought fewer women into the workforce.

In other words, they are experiencing the same shifts in the structure of production and employment as the US and UK, but at a far slower pace. The benefits of delay have accrued to male workers and company owners in traditional manufacturing industries, while the implict costs have been borne by female labour market 'outsiders' and anybody creating businesses in non-traditional sectors.

The trouble with ignoring such evidence on basically ideological grounds is that, by default, denying reality leaves the shaping of that reality open to others. There is therefore an urgent need for progressive policies for Europe that embrace fundamental economic change as an opportunity to shape a better society in future, rather than seeing it as a threat to what is, after all, a hugely flawed society now. Is there a European model so successful that it is worth defending in exactly its present form at any price? The answer has to be no.

For it is simply not true that there is only one other model available. The American version of the new economy has been shaped by that country's history, culture and political priorities; Europe could not import and install it wholesale even if it wanted to.

New opportunities to create a different model appropriate to a European context are offered by several trends. These include the continuing change in the international structure of production, the crumbling of hierarchical methods of organization, the development of network organizations and increased social and economic mobility.

Any change is of course enormously disruptive, and is bound to result in some groups losing out. The experience of deindustrialization in all our countries has been that government policies for cushioning the losers are utterly inadequate.

Yet there is nothing intrinsically worth preserving about many or most of the traditional factory jobs that have been lost since the mid-1970s. They were boring, uncomfortable or even dangerous, badly paid and put management firmly in control of employees. The working class communities formed around such employment tend to be over-romanticized, which is all the easier to do now that so few remain.

With a different lens, eliminating all these jobs would look to be a desirable policy ambition – if only they could all be done by machines. The catch is that the workers involved were often left without other employment and income when the jobs vanished.

Conventional policies have been hugely unimaginative. They have focused on compensating organizations rather than individuals. For example, one common response is for governments to give funds to companies on the basis of promises (rarely monitored) about creating jobs or preserving jobs in particular places, a strategy sure only to postpone the inevitable outcome. Or local councils have received the funds, to be spent with varying degrees of wisdom and scrutiny, even in cases like mining villages where it is clear that the local geographic basis for economic activity has vanished.

Policy-makers must focus in future on people, not places; and on individuals, not organizations, whether companies, unions or local political units. The aim must be not just to provide benefits, as these will always be lower than the income work would provide, but rather to provide access to work. This might involve paying for training, but equally it might involve buying a house that has become worthless so that an unemployed person can move without crystallizing a loss on his or her biggest asset, or it might be a matter of making pension contributions for a period, or buying a car to allow someone to commute.

Other policies too need to focus on enabling individual choices. Pensions are a key area for reform. The ageing populations in Europe mean a truly fundamental rethink of pensions is desirable – is it right for tax policy to distort people's choices so firmly in favour of taking all their leisure when they are over 60, when it might now be appropriate to encourage very late retirement via a winding-down period of part-time work, and also when so many younger people struggle financially to achieve a better work-life balance?

Besides, nowhere in Europe are pensions really seen as individual assets that are fully portable and over which their owners ought to be able to exercise a high degree of choice. The control still lies mainly with companies or public sector employers; but they are not a satisfactory channel for managing an individual's retirement income when there is now such a great likelihood that any person will have changed employers several times in a working life, and moved in and out of employment for any number of reasons, or perhaps lived abroad.

Indeed, these are increasingly less appropriate bodies for the delivery of any kind of government policy, whether it is tax collection or the administration of sickness or maternity or other benefits and tax credits. The typical company now will not survive for as long as the typical working life. Nobody entering the labour force now expects to stay with the same employer for a full career. Using employers as a delivery mechanism for government policy clearly penalizes 'outsiders' in the labour market, whether they are mothers, young people, unskilled workers stuck in transient jobs or illegal immigrants – in other words, all the more vulnerable groups which ought to be priorities for a progressive policy framework. Equally, it privileges 'insider' groups, especially union members in corporatist economies. (While clearly doing a good job in protecting their own members, unions represent one of the most powerful vested interests in the workplace with which vulnerable groups have to contend.)

Similarly, while better corporate governance is important, it is never going to transform society. Private sector companies are a key element of the economy, but not more than they have been in the past. The idea that untramelled corporate power is circumscribing our lives more than ever is pure myth. The mechanisms by which this is supposed to have happened are never spelt out by anti-corporate critics. (Do they force consumers to buy an unwanted mountain of designer sneakers? Do they subvert the competition authorities? Have they successfully reduced the amount of regulation by government? The answer to all of these is 'no'.) The facts are that the share of GDP accounted for by government rather than private sector companies has been rising everywhere outside the former communist bloc, and that companies (like individuals) have been paying more tax rather than less to finance this expansion of government. And big corporations, like any other established source of authority in the modern world, feel that they are losing control. As they all are.

So building a fairer society is still going to depend more on shaping government policies than reforming corporate behaviour. And there are many other areas of policy where there is vast scope for progressive measures that transfer control over people's lives to the individuals themselves, away from their employers and indeed elected politicians and unelected officials. Some of these have a familiar flavour and are politically comfortable – the vexed area of work-life balance is one. Another is the importance of equipping individuals with the kind of education that gives them access to all kinds of opportunities and equips them to cope with dramatic economic change, better education, more of it, and continuing access through their lives.

Others are less comfortable because they appear on the face of it to derive from the free market tradition – for example, choice amongst providers of public services is exactly this kind of issue in the UK. The difficulty is that many traditionally progressive public sector unions are precisely the kind of bureaucratic hierarchy that is being undermined in the new economy. The public sector across Europe lags far behind the corporate sector in starting to adjust to the diffusion of control and switch away from hierarchical towards network organizations.

Centralized state delivery cannot survive, though, and it is important to take active steps now to shape the public sector and public policies of the future rather than wasting effort preserving a public sector formed out of the philosophies and struggles of the mid-20th century.

For government, underpinning market institutions is just as important as ever to capitalist economies – in fact more so in the new variety where economic value is added primarily through human interactions. The ways in which we all mediate our relationships with each other, the structures for resolving conflict between groups, the legal framework – in short, all that is encompassed in the idea of government – are more important than ever. Let's not miss the chance to improve by regarding the new economy as an irrelevance or a threat rather than a once in a century opportunity.

Europe's Enterprise Strategy

Wendy Alexander, [former] Minister for Enterprise, Lifelong Learning and Transport, Scottish Executive

INTRODUCTION

The role of politicians is perhaps different post 11 September 2001 than it was before. Up until now it was perhaps too easy to take what we have for granted. When our society and way of life is under threat we dwell on its strengths and achievements.

Let us not forget that the economic successes of western civilization speak for themselves: built on democracy, the rule of law, effective government institutions, sound macro-economic policy and a liberal tradition. We already have what economists call the 'social capital' that underpins our economic success. Many, many parts of the world don't have this advantage. This is not the place to pose the question of whether we are at the 'end of history' or in a 'clash of civilizations'. Let us be more prosaic – we have in Europe the economic tradition and a society that is right for us and which, in present circumstances, will need to be defended.

But as politicians we need the modesty and sure-footedness to recognize that the economy of Europe, our social circumstances, health and environment are not perfect – far from it. There is more we can do – which will require a positive and constructive role for governments at local, national and supra-national level. Our task is to:

- cultivate the pre-conditions of economic success
- promote the achievement of that success
- clear up the legacy of past policy mistakes.

NATIONS AND REGIONS

My particular interest is of course to emphasize the experience of nations and regions within Europe. A supra-national policy approach can complement our national and sub-national strategies, but must also respond to the voices from across all of Europe.

With devolution, my country – Scotland – has gained a new voice. The decisions we take now will affect our children and grandchildren: the kind of Scotland they live in and the kind of world they live in. It is a great responsibility and a great opportunity.

Like any country undertaking such a bold political experiment, we are on a steep learning curve. A new political culture is emerging, and there is more open debate in Scotland about Scottish issues. We are learning, not least the politicians, about what are the right things to do and about how to do things right.

FUNDAMENTAL AIMS

We see the objectives of an enterprise policy as being to enhance the success and well-being of:

- our businesses
- our people
- our communities.

Why our businesses? Well, the evidence is clear. The UK has a sizeable productivity gap, compared with France/Germany and, especially, the USA. And Scotland's performance is slightly below that of the UK as a whole. Within UK manufacturing, the most productive plants are $5^{1}/_{2}$ times as productive as the least productive plants.

In Scotland (as in the UK), there is, as yet, little evidence of the new economy in the official statistics on productivity. The central theme must be to improve productivity across the whole economy.

Why our people? The Labour government made a promise on the right to work. And in moving back to full employment we are closer than at any time in my lifetime. But we didn't just promise to put people back to work: the second promise we made was to make that work pay.

Labour is about making sure all Scots are ready for tomorrow's jobs, not just the young Scots, not just the highly educated Scots, not just the go-ahead Scots – but all Scots. I would commend that principle to you as the mission for any enterprise strategy.

Why our communities? Remember the Thatcherite doctrine that 'there is no such thing as society, only individuals'. How misguided that was. We now see prosperous and empowered communities as the essential prerequisite, as well as desirable product, of successful economies. This means that wider social, environmental, health and legal policies can each contribute to successful economies. As Geoff Mulgan noted, the synergies between these policies are a profound driver of economic well-being. At the risk of simplifying matters, we need to move forward recognizing that a strong economy can make for a better society, and empowered communities aid a strong economy.

FRAMEWORK FOR BUSINESS

So how can we achieve these aims? Above all, politicians can provide the framework for business to flourish, including:

- sound macro-economic policies
- strong and effective competition
- effective micro-economic interventions
- reduced barriers on business growth
- complementary and mutually reinforcing social, environmental and economic policy.

This is a challenge that will require the modernization of institutions and clarity in a policy approach.

We in Scotland have made strides in this direction in recent years, and let me outline some of these.

GLOBAL CONNECTIONS

For a small country, Scotland has had an incredible influence on the world. In the early 20th century the Scots gave the world the telephone, the television, the fax machine, the video recorder and radar.

While Scots continue to make their way successfully overseas, we want to improve significantly our international performance in a rapidly changing and increasingly open global economy. Hence our new Global Connections Strategy to provide the platform for achieving this goal.

Our new strategy recognizes that the world has moved on to the era of the knowledge economy. We're shifting our focus from concentrating solely on exports and securing inward investment to concentrating on knowledge, with three main priorities:

- The first priority is knowledge out of Scotland – helping companies exploit Scottish knowledge through partnerships and commercialization of academic research and development.
- The second priority area is knowledge in. By this I mean helping companies utilize Scottish knowledge in Scotland.
- The third priority area is people. We live in an age where skills and knowledge, not low cost, are our key competitive weapons. We therefore need to ensure we have an open economy, which promotes the exchange of skills and networking of individuals from Scotland and the rest of the world.

As part of our new strategy we have created a new organization, Scottish Development International, that integrates and extends the range of our current overseas activities. Our vision is for a fully integrated world-wide organization that brings Scotland to the world and the world to Scotland.

ENTERPRISE CULTURE

Entrepreneurs are an industrious breed of people, often recorded in history for their inspiration and inventiveness and for the everyday tools and techniques which we take for granted today. We need a continuous stream of such inspired individuals to drive our economic growth and our society's prosperity: through their innovation; their development of products and processes; their pursuit of market opportunities, both at home and abroad; their 'never say impossible' attitude; and the vision that they bring.

All this should be self-evident. But for some reason, today's society fails to acknowledge properly their achievements, and the contribution they make to our wealth and prosperity. We need to change society's attitudes towards entrepreneurship: first by acknowledging the achievements being made by such individuals, and then by encouraging and assisting others to follow their example.

It is therefore right that we should catch them young – primary schools (and even the enterprising approaches applied in pre-school) are the ideal starting-blocks from which the torch of enterprise will be lit.

LEARNING AND SKILLS

We must foster the ideals of lifelong learning, encouraging society as a whole to participate in a learning culture. After all, learning is the key to earning.

Preparing people for employment is high on our agenda. Scotland's future economic success will require the skills and training needs of employers and individuals to be clearly identified, developed and met if we are to ensure that every Scot is ready for the jobs of tomorrow. Together, we need to improve the operation of the Scottish labour market, narrow the gap in unemployment rates across Scotland, provide the best start for all our young people and improve the matching of people to jobs.

We cannot offer individuals a safety net, but we can offer them a trampoline by providing opportunities for everyone to update their skills. We have to knock down barriers to learning and change the old concept that learners have to fit in with the courses available, whether this is convenient for them or not. We need to put the learner, not the provider, first.

These goals can best be achieved by more accurately forecasting future skills needs and providing the appropriate learning opportunities to guide individuals to meet the challenge of change successfully. The establishment of Future Skills Scotland and the move to an all-age Careers Scotland will facilitate this.

UNIVERSITIES

If you go back 50 years to just after the war, 1 in 10 went on to higher education in Scotland. By 1970, and a Labour government committed to the Robins' expansion, it was 2 in 10. By 1980 it was 3 in 10; by the mid-1990s it was 4 in 10. Today it is 47% of Scottish youngsters. During this Parliament, it will exceed 1 in 2.

Still only 1 in 10 of our university entrants come from families of 'D' and 'E' social status. This becomes more and more important at a time when what you learn is more and more related to what you earn.

But in Scotland over the last few years we have tended to confuse student financial support with the future of our universities. They are different issues. The real importance of higher education to Scotland is that it is the source of the intellectual assets upon which our future depends.

Scottish universities are at the heart of our ability to have a knowledge education of the future, literally to transform the gross rate from the historic 2.5% towards the rates we have seen in Ireland of 8, 9 and 10%.

That sort of transformation will not be achieved by the £0.5 billion that we spend on Scottish Enterprise and Highlands & Islands Enterprise. It will only be achieved if we can ensure that the £0.5 billion spent on Scottish Enterprise works alongside the £0.5 billion that will now be spent on further education and the more than £0.5 billion spent on higher education.

In the future, we need to do things differently: better management, better priorities, new incentives and reward structures. Such change is never easy, but Scotland's future may, quite literally, depend on it and the 8% rise in expenditure on education in 2001 is a signal to those in the sector to grasp the opportunities.

In the 18th century the Scottish Enlightenment, nurtured in our universities, provided the underpinning for Scottish wealth in the 19th century. And so, for Scotland, our investment in our universities throughout the 20th century can be the basis for prosperity in the 21st century.

The significance of the global assets locked up in our universities is well known. In Stanford they talked about Edinburgh's expertise in voice recognition and the large number of joint citations between Stanford and Edinburgh academics. In biotechnology the expertise of Sir David Lane and Philip Cohen have attracted eight of the top ten pharmaceutical companies to that city. Universities are at the heart of our enterprise economy.

CONCLUSIONS

My key messages for the enterprise strategy are:

- Learn from experience across Europe – small nations and large, regions and areas.
- Draw in the wider community – schools, the education system, welfare policies all have a big role to play.
- Identify what can be done at a European level and what needs to be done at the level of local communities.
- Look for synergies across policies.
- Modernize and adopt the public sector economic development effort.
- Above all, look to knowledge and the universities as drivers of economic change.

Taming Prometheus

How to build the 'value-values' economy

John Philpott, Chartered Institute of Personnel and Development

WHY PROMETHEUS MUST BE TAMED

Irony abounds in today's global society. Anti-western terrorists deploy capitalist management techniques to commit mass murder. Anti-capitalist protesters use Dell and Microsoft technology to co-ordinate their actions. And anti-corporate radicals rally to their own international brand, No Logo.

Why is the same free market society that makes all this possible the source of such hostility? The answer of course is that Prometheus has, in the past generation, broken free of the chains that once constrained him. The architects of the immediate post-1945 settlement understood that market forces could both transform and destroy the socio-economic landscape. An active public policy regime was thus needed to preserve the common good in the face of any tendency to capitalist excess. Sadly, this truth got lost in the ideological battle between socialism in all its totalitarian forms and a peculiarly narrow version of neo-liberal economics. The victory of the latter was thus not accompanied by any post-Cold War settlement, with finance and profit taking precedence over the wider needs of society.

The consequences have been profound: high rates of structural joblessness, relative deprivation and wrecked communities blight affluent western consumer societies. Rampant capitalism meanwhile spreads throughout the Third World, bringing advanced technology and raising average incomes but with little respect for ancient traditions and no apparent concern for either the abject poverty of the unskilled masses or the natural environment. The backlash – whether in the form of street protest or violent terror – is now well underway. But religious fundamentalism and Green-Left luddism, of the kind that smashes its way through the world's major cities, itself represents a threat to the open society. The common good instead requires a political economy that seeks to socialize, rather than oppose, the market – Prometheus tamed but allowed to express his power.

Such a political economy cannot, however, be constructed on the remnants of 20th century social democracy. As so-called 'Third Way' commentators have rightly emphasized, public policy institutions must be aligned to the prevailing psychology of individual self-expression and its market corollary, mass customization. Any other approach will neither gain sufficient political legitimacy nor be economically successful.

People today ask for freedom to be themselves in civil society, and choice and value in the market-place. If it is to succeed in making the market work for society, the state cannot therefore be overtly *controlling* and bureaucratic. Its new role must be to influence the market by means of altering economic incentives and enabling emergent progressive social attitudes to change consumer behaviour and alter business priorities. In other words, policy-makers must harness the same market processes that require organizations to add greater value to goods and services in ways that ensure that organizations adopt decent values with regard to all the economic, social and natural environments in which they operate.

Increased discussion of Corporate Social Responsibility (CSR) indicates some welcome movement in this direction. But despite talk of a new stakeholder model of European enterprise, the maximization of shareholder value is, if anything, a more overt priority for European businesses than ever before. As a result, the purely ethical case for CSR is inevitably giving way to the business case as expressed in such ideas as 'triple bottom line' accounting (ie accounting that takes note of profits, people and the environment). This represents the best route to a new policy approach to European enterprise. The underlying objective must be to build what might be called the 'value-values' economy, with public policy designed to maximize the power and influence of individuals over organizations both as consumers and employees. In contrast to the illiberal and prescriptive stance of the anti-globalization lobby, this approach amounts to using competitive market forces to themselves channel the market in positive directions.

THE 'VALUE-VALUES' ECONOMY

The potential to build a truly 'value-values' economy in Europe can be identified from emergent trends in the product and labour markets of developed western economies.

Consumers, aided by new, cheaper forms of information technology, notably the internet, nowadays have greater market power. They have more sophisticated tastes and shop around in national and international markets as well as local markets. They may seek low prices and value for money but they also place a premium on intangibles like design, brands and the 'ethical content' of what they purchase. They are also more willing to switch product loyalty under the influence of multi-media advertising, 'life-style' broadcasting and documentaries or investigative reports about the way in which organizations operate in terms of employment conditions or environmental impacts etc.

As a result, product market competition is more intense in the private sector regardless of whether a business is exposed to global or purely domestic competitive pressures. Moreover, competition is also affecting relations between organizations and those with whom they collaborate at the various intermediate stages in the process of meeting consumer demand. Organizations are establishing more intricate relationships with purchasers, suppliers and contractors to engineer production and delivery structures that both keep costs in check and improve product or service quality. The result is more out-sourcing and, increasingly, more business to business e-commerce as organizations make use of rapidly developing information and communications technologies to establish virtual supply chains, often transcending traditional geographical boundaries.

This is what the 'new global economy' really means; not a distinct group of internet-based dot.com companies but a set of new global economic relations. But the key factor here is not so much the advanced technology as the competitive pressure that this instils. Although the anti-globalization movement is built on the justifiable concern that the internationalization of investment, trade and mass marketing operates to the detriment of the world's disadvantaged communities, the very competition that this generates offers consumers more power than ever before to influence organizations at every point along local, national and international supply chains.

Organizations thus have to ensure that they are seen to be clean players in relation to the what, where and how of their activities; if not, consumers will desert them for competitors able to provide better value and/or who demonstrate better values. Moreover, a poor corporate reputation – whether in terms of product and service quality or ethical behaviour – can travel through the supply chain like a virus. Each link in the chain thus has an interest in making sure that both it and its collaborators remain in touch and in tune with consumer desires.

At the same time the labour market pressures facing employers are also becoming more intense. On the demand side, heightened product market competition is placing a premium on recruiting, developing and managing people whose skills and knowledge can enable organizations to secure a competitive quality advantage. Hence the frequent references in management school speak to a 'war for talent'. In addition, a value shift is taking place on the supply side of the labour market. Individuals who expect a high quality deal from organizations as consumers of goods and services are increasingly looking for a similar deal as workers too. This helps explain the tendency for the concept of 'pay' to give way to that of 'reward' – reflecting the desire of workers to forgo simple cash payment in favour of shares in their organization, or a range of non-monetary benefits (eg free heath insurance) etc.

Even more significant, however, is that the various dimensions of reward are becoming increasingly complex. Workers preoccupied with 'time sovereignty' and 'work-life balance' may prefer to trade money for time in their reward package, raising their hourly pay rather than boosting their weekly income. Likewise, individuals are more likely to include corporate reputation – or 'employer brand' – in the matrix of monetary and non-monetary factors that determine their choice of where to work. Once a satisfactory base level of monetary income is secured the level of 'psychic' or 'ethical' income on offer is nowadays likely to be the clincher; a trend highlighted in particular by professional recruitment agencies. Consequently, organizations that do not offer a decent reward package, provide opportunities for employee development and meet aspirations for an improved work-life balance or ethical considerations may not be able to guarantee the calibre of worker they need to match market competitors.

BUILDING THE 'VALUE-VALUES' ECONOMY

The combination of these product market and labour market developments is placing organizations under increasing pressure to raise their game. This is ultimately likely to prove a far more significant determinant of change in organizational behaviour – acting as it does directly upon shareholder interest – than elaborate expositions of stakeholder capitalism. The key to creating the latter is thus to empower stakeholders where they can best make their influence felt, ie in the market-place. In other words, market forces are themselves the best defence against capitalist excess.

However, the consumer and worker empowerment needed to ensure that the market serves, rather than undermines, the common good is not guaranteed automatically within the free market. The neo-liberal deification of the unfettered market – especially that which stems from Hayek's Austrian school – sweeps aside the evident failures in the market system, identified by pragmatic economists of different political persuasions since the Keynesian revolution of the 1930s. A value-values economy within Europe would therefore need to be underpinned by a variety of policy instruments. Principal amongst these are macro-economic and employment policies directed at the preservation of full employment, plus business policy measures that aim to maximize product market competition.

High unemployment – whether due to structural causes or deficient demand – always represents the biggest obstacle to economic, social and environmental progress. Full employment was the major European casualty of the ideological battle between free market fundamentalism and mid-20th century social democracy. The failure of the old school European social democrats to maintain high and stable levels of employment without generating inflation was followed by growing acceptance of passive welfare dependence in the 1980s and most of the 1990s.

Mass joblessness, and the income inequality associated with it, limits the power of individuals to place pressure on organizations within the labour market and creates a disadvantaged core of restricted consumers within society, with no alternative but to purchase solely on the basis of price. As a consequence, production and working practices based on value and values is rendered a purely strategic or enlightened choice rather than an organizational necessity; shoddy goods and poor treatment of stakeholders tend to be widespread. It should come as no surprise, therefore, that the fuller employment enjoyed in the United States and the UK during the long-boom of the 1990s coincided with the trend towards greater emphasis on corporate reputation and employer brand. This makes it vital that European macro-economic and welfare policies are continually geared to the maintenance of full employment; especially during periods of global economic turbulence.

The conclusion that full employment is a central plank of a progressive society should be delivered loud and clear to those Green-Left radicals who, at times, appear to view mistaken 'end of work' theories as somehow good news. But full employment in a numerical sense is clearly not enough. A value-values labour market is one in which all workers and jobseekers are sufficiently empowered to secure a better deal from employers; which means improving the number of people with transferable skills that are in demand and enhancing the so-called 'psychological contract' within the workplace.

Increasing the supply of required transferable skills will enable a faster rate of growth in productivity, stimulate a rise in income and put more product and labour market pressure on business. It is arguable that this itself would encourage more employers voluntarily to develop a better psychological contract, reducing the need for tougher legislation on workers' rights as stakeholders. In practice, however, the state would of course have to guarantee a set of minimum workplace standards and perhaps maintain the threat of raising these if progress on the voluntary front is slow. The state might also provide tax incentives or credits to organizations that engage in progressive training or people management practices, such as, for example, employee share ownership schemes which appear to encourage 'shared interest' organizations and boost workplace productivity. But what should be required by law is greater transparency of organizational practice towards all internal and external stakeholders. Company reporting should, in particular, highlight the range of people management and human capital practices undertaken. This would not only demonstrate to actual and potential employees the underlying strength of the employer brand, but would also act as a financial market signal to shareholders of the likely ability of organizations to succeed in the 'talent war' and thus boost shareholder value.

Full employment and better working practices will doubtless appeal to Europe's traditional social democrats. Less immediately appealing to such an audience – but an equally important condition of a value-values economy – is the necessity to foster within Europe a US-style entrepreneurial culture. Budding entrepreneurs in the US find it easier to obtain venture capital than their EU counterparts and face a regulatory regime that makes it relatively easy to set-up and operate businesses. This helps to increase the contestability and competitiveness of US product markets, adds to consumer choice, helps boost productivity and probably explains why US employment rates are far higher than those of the EU in all parts of the emerging service sector, high and low skilled.

There are of course well known down-sides to the US approach to business – not least, concern about the environmental impacts of light planning regulation. However, it is by no means clear that regulation is the best means of securing environmental improvement. Although progress is slow, US consumers are already beginning to exert more pressure on organizations to become greener. Europe would probably want to move faster. But even within a European context it would be generally more appropriate to use green taxes, rather than regulation, as the main anti-pollution tool, with any additional revenues redirected to environmentally friendly job creation projects in the social economy. The combination of market pressure and financial incentives is nearly always preferable to bureaucrat diktat; the latter alone tends to result in excessive red tape and at best minimum compliance.

IS EUROPE READY?

What are the prospects of European policy-makers creating the kind of competitive, full employment Europe needed to secure the value-values economy? In fact, quite promising. The picture drawn by free market zealots – especially in the UK – of a sclerotic, over-regulated and high un-employment Europe is no more than a caricature. It conveys elements of truth, certainly, but is a distortion nonetheless. The basic European model has its strengths and weaknesses, as does its Anglo-American peer. But variations on the basic model observed in individual EU member states have proved very successful in terms of growth, employment, productivity and social cohesion. Moreover, despite the continuing democratic deficit – which makes EU level decision-making appear remote and complicated to the mass of European voters – the EU has proved capable of constructing an economic policy framework suited to the needs of the early 21st century.

The establishment of the euro currency, the completion of the single market and the developing European Employment Strategy with its four policy pillars and related guidelines represent all the elements necessary. The only question mark is over implementation. On macro-economic policy, the European Central Bank's inflexible inflation target and the overly restrictive fiscal stability pact that underlies EMU are a remnant of 1980s monetarist orthodoxy. Neither feature of the macro-policy framework is friendly to full employment and both need to be reformed. The relatively robust performance of the UK economy in the wake of the world economic downturn in 2001 clearly demonstrates the advantages of a symmetrical inflation target and a more responsive fiscal policy regime. On structural policy the problem, as ever in Europe, is one of ensuring that grand policy initiatives are implemented swiftly and effectively.

Assuming sensible movement on both fronts, the European enterprise outlook is promising. More organizations will be subject to the value-values pressures that will push them towards triple bottom line accounting. Prometheus can be tamed. All that stands in the way of this are the forces of conservatism on both the left and right of the European political spectrum. Free market fundamentalism remains strong, while the anti-globalization movement seems determined to prevent democratically elected politicians from meeting to discuss the best way forward. Of the two, the latter at present seems to pose the bigger threat, having no clearly articulated political agenda other than opposition to 'the system' for opposition's sake. As mentioned at the outset, today's world is rife with irony. What greater irony than that those who claim to speak for the world's disadvantaged, and say that they wish to preserve its very existence as an ecosystem, end up as the main barrier to a better tomorrow.

Building A Sustainable Networked Knowledge Society In Europe

Peter Johnston, the European Commission

The agreement in Gothenburg to link the European strategy for sustainable development to the 'Lisbon Strategy', and the transition to a dynamic knowledge-based economy, puts the further development and use of networking technologies at the heart of an integrated policy for growth, employment, social cohesion and sustainable development.

Yet, while there is a sound conceptual basis for a networked knowledge economy to be more sustainable, there are still few policy initiatives and frameworks in place to make this a reality.

The key challenge is to realize a more sustainable level of resource use in a re-engineered and networked 'knowledge society', rather than simply (and inadequately) in a 'cleaner' industrial society.

The key requirement and opportunities are firstly in research:

1. To better understand the opportunities for improved efficiencies in business and transport logistics that can reduce resource use and add value to a wide range of goods and services
2. To understand the opportunities and limits to immaterialization through the substitution of e-services for manufactured goods
3. To understand and monitor how changes in land use, city planning, office design and work organization can reduce resource use and improve the quality of life.

While governments (at both EU and national level) can set the general objectives and frameworks for change, the burden of realizing change must rest on businesses and individuals. The key frameworks for progress will therefore be those for Corporate Social Responsibility (CSR) and for citizen-led action. There must therefore be a strong linkage to the enterprise strategy for Europe.

The European Commission has initiated a wide debate on new approaches to sustainable development at the Gothenburg Summit. It has proposed a new framework for European research and technology development, focused on the twin themes of the 'knowledge economy' and 'sustainable development'. The Commission has launched a wide consultation on CSR and supports efforts by the world-leading IT and telecommunications companies to define practical 'triple bottom line' reporting guidelines for the knowledge economy.

The Commission is also working with the Club of Rome and the 'Factor 10 Club' to establish target scenarios for a sustainable knowledge society and road-maps for research and technology development.

From this work so far, the three specific recommendations for successful implementation of these scenarios are:

1. To re-emphasize and sustain the rapid deployment of high-speed network access in every community in Europe.
2. To systematically seek higher added value and greater efficiency in *all* resource use (land, energy, transport and materials) in all business and government activities.
3. To sustain investments in human capital through lifelong learning for all; in social capital through peer-to-peer network developments; and in our cultural capital through promotion of diversity and creativity.

SECTION 4

Making Progressive Enterprise Work

'… Progress, man's distinctive mark alone…'

A Death in the Desert, Robert Browning, 1864

Measuring Progressivity

The Calvert-Henderson quality of life indicators

Hazel Henderson, Calvert Henderson

The Calvert-Henderson Quality of Life Indicators (C-HQLI) are the fulfilment of 25 years of effort, research and advocacy in the USA and world-wide for more comprehensive statistics beyond the traditional macro-economic indicators, GNP/GDP based on the United Nations System of National Accounts (UNSNA). Since 11 September the need for sharper, broader tools for assessing national trends has become even more urgent. For example, our National Security Indicator was calling for new emphasis on diplomacy, treaty ratification and intelligence to deal with cyber warfare, terrorism and new threats. The proliferation of alternative measures of sustainable human development and quality of life attest to tremendous progress in the past decade. The United Nations Development Project's (UNDP) first Human Development Index (HDI) in 1990, devised by the late Mahbub ul Haq and UNDP's current Director of Development Studies, Inge Kaul, gave all our efforts great impetus.

After many years of presenting and debating such expanded approaches to national accounts with government and academic colleagues at venues world-wide, I found a 'fit' with the research needs of a leading, innovative socially responsible investment firm located in the United States, The Calvert Group of Bethesda, MD. Calvert has been in the mutual fund management business for 25 years and manages approximately US$7.0 billion in assets in 27 screened and non-screened portfolios for over 220,000 shareholders.

Calvert's responsible investment practices are based on the belief that caring for our natural environment and recognizing the importance of human dignity is essential to the long-term health and well-being of our increasingly interdependent world. In the early 1980s, Calvert pioneered the use of social investing on a broader scale than ever before. In 1982, the Calvert Social Investment Fund became the first mutual fund to oppose apartheid in South Africa. Fittingly, in 1994, following Nelson Mandela's victory in the country's first open elections, Calvert became one of the first mutual funds to reinvest in a free South Africa. Calvert recognizes that investing in companies that are committed to meeting the challenges of the future with an expanded view of corporate responsibility is more than just a matter of 'doing the right thing' – it also makes good business sense. Calvert embraces the concept that a primary objective of every corporation should be to enhance the wealth of all stakeholders, not just the company's shareholders, but also its employees, customers, vendors, communities and the natural environment. More than US$2 trillion is invested today in the United States in a socially responsible manner, according to a study released in 1999 by the US non-profit Social Investment Forum.

The C-HQLI project was launched in 1994 by Calvert's Social Investment Research Department, directed by Jon Lickerman. Why does a private sector financial firm publish such a set of indicators of quality of life? I will quote directly from Calvert Group's CEO, Barbara Krumsiek:

'All over the country, citizens are demonstrating a desire to engage in serious discussions about how to measure quality of life and liveable communities in the United States. For the past five years, Calvert Group has been preparing for this exciting debate. We are pleased to release in this initial volume the Calvert-Henderson Quality of Life Indicators, the first national, comprehensive assessment of the quality of life in the United States using a systems approach. The deep insights, illuminating findings and bold explorations into historical and contemporary environmental, economic and social conditions of the country are our contributions to this important debate. We hope its messages and many lessons will empower people from all walks of life who are equally con-cerned about our future together on this planet.'[1]

Beyond this social mission of educating investors and the general public, other factors are important. As Jon Lickerman, now Chair of the Advisory Board, says:

'Over the course of our practice in socially responsible investing, it became evident that there were no broad indicators by which to guide our unique investment strategy. Yes, our managers had traditional eco-nomic indicators to help guide their financial investment decisions. Routine releases of the Consumer Price Index, housing starts, consumer credit, manufacturing orders and capacity utilization, job vacancies, growth in average earnings, productivity and unit labor costs all pro-vide information to navigate the direction of economic cycles and investment strategies.

As a leading practitioner in the field of socially responsible invest-ing, Calvert analysts did not have tools similar to those available to tra-ditional investment professionals. We understood the need for a broader array of socio-economic indicators. We also began to understand that there was little information available to understand the relationships between economic forces and societal or environmental impacts. This dilemma led Calvert into the field of quality of life indicators. How was it that we could analyze the environmental impact of a major chemi-cal company, yet we could not ascertain the overall quality of the envi-ronment in which it operates? In the fast food industry, analysts had no indicators that would elucidate how further investments in an inher-ently low wage industry might impact broader socio-economic trends. What were the trends in national income distribution? What were the demographics of this traditionally low wage segment of the workforce? Was this growth industry contributing to increased national income

---

[1] *The Calvert-Henderson Quality of Life Indicators: a new tool for assessing national trends*, Eds. Hazel Henderson, Jon Lickerman, Patrice Flynn, Calvert Group Inc, Bethesda, MD, 2000 p. 1

disparities or simply providing a low rung step in the ladder of economic development for workers?'[2]

Indeed, Calvert Group frequently finds it necessary to undertake such broader, quality of life research on issues of emerging concerns to their shareholders and society, for example, privacy, biotechnology and genetic engineering, impacts of commercialism and mass media on children. Similarly, the screening process (both positive and negative) of corporations for inclusion in Calvert's mutual fund portfolios is constantly refined. For example, Calvert does not invest in companies that are involved in weapons production, nuclear energy, or that are out of compliance with environmental regulations, core labour standards or are involved in human rights violations or disputes with indigenous peoples. Calvert's 'positive screens' seek innovative companies that create social benefits and environmental remediation and are geared towards sustainable use of energy and resources. Indeed, as Calvert's Social Research Department has broadened its research since Calvert Group's founding 25 years ago, this huge knowledge base is increasingly sought after by outside entities including traditional financial firms, and increasingly, academia, government agencies, public officials and Civic Society Organizations (CSOs).

The C-HQLI measure conditions and trends in 12 key socio-economic sectors of the USA based on my Country Futures Indicators (CFI) model (Henderson, 1991, 1995), co-created by myself and the Calvert Group.[3] These Indicators were developed over five years under the guidance of Hazel Henderson, Jon Lickerman and Patrice Flynn (President, Flynn Research, Harpers Ferry, WV), and a team of experts in each of the 12 Indicator domains: Education, Jill Dianne Swenson; Employment, Patrice Flynn; Energy, John A 'Skip' Laitner; Environment, Kenneth P Scott; Health,

---

[2] ibid, p. 17. The Calvert Group's Jon Lickerman can be contacted at www.calvert.com. Hazel Henderson is at www.hazelhenderson.com and Patrice Flynn at www.flynnresearch.com
[3] Reference manual for the Calvert-Henderson Quality of Life Indicators is available from Amazon.com; hazelhenderson.com or from the Calvert Group, PO box 30348, Bethesda, MD 20814; paperback US$25.00 including postage

Constance Battle and Mary Jenifer; Human Rights, Alya Kayal; Income, Lawrence Mishel; Infrastructure, Will Mallett; National Security, Colonel Daniel M Smith; Public Safety, Trudy A Karlson; Re-creation, Richard Peterson and Carrie Lee; Shelter, Patrick Simmons. US population/demographic data cross-cuts through all 12 Indicators. Population increases show, by most forecasts, a rise of between 8 and 10 billion people on our planet early in this new millennium. However, the huge global gap between rich and poor still shows that per capita consumption of energy and resources in the US is some 50 times greater than that of some 2 billion of the world's poor and under-nourished. Thus, the most potent threat to the environment is waste and over consumption, with the US as the world's chief polluter. The other Indicators show the potential for redesigning infrastructures and production methods using better information and how 'greener technologies' can also benefit the world's climate and ecology – as well as quality of life.

The 12 Indicators were selected using many sources. First, they are major areas of public concern as reflected in public opinion polls, the media, political campaigns and debates over decades. Secondly, these domains are most often covered in many of the existing sets of local, state, national and international statistics we reviewed. Each one of our Indicators allows revealing insights which are often invisible in highly averaged indices.

In two separate polls on governmental reform by the highly respected Americans Talk Issues Foundation, Americans were asked if they approved or disapproved of the following proposal:

'In the same way we've developed and used the Gross National Product to measure the growth of the economy, [we should] develop and use a scorecard of new indicators for holding politicians responsible for progress toward other national goals, like improving education, extending health care, preserving the environment and making the military meet today's needs.'

In these two surveys of March 1993, 72% of the American people agreed that such quality of life indicators were needed. These results were verified in a debate format where an opposing view was offered in the second survey in January of 1994:

'Opponents say that eventually economists will be able to calculate a single indicator of progress, a kind of enlarged GNP, that bundles into this money-based statistic our progress in all major areas including the economy, health, education, the environment and so forth. This single number would be easier for everyone to use to rank ourselves against other nations and to judge the performance of our political leaders.'

Only 22% of respondents found this opposing view to be convincing, and when the original question was asked again, support went up to 79%.[4]

The Calvert-Henderson model presents the first systems approach to measuring quality of life.[5] The Indicators are unbundled for full transparency and public education, but are conceptually linked and interfaced in the overall model. Each Indicator domain is mapped by a sub-system model describing the relationships between institutional structures and how decisions flow through the sector to create outcomes (measured by the most reliable, official and academic statistics). Each Indicator domain uses appropriate metrics and disciplines for its data-streams. Baseline evaluations of existing statistics and methods identify their changing relevance to each evolving socio-economic sector and highlight statistical 'blind spots'.

The use of macro-economic aggregation and weighting formulae is deliberately avoided, so as to minimize distortion and opacity. This systems methodology serves both the purposes of public education and the needs of asset managers in constructing socially responsible portfolios according to social criteria and performance of companies in all of the 12 Indicator domains. An important goal is to help improve the quality and breadth of existing national statistics.

[4] Kay, Alan F, *Locating Consensus for Democracy*, Americans Talk Issues Foundation, St. Augustine, FL (1998)
[5] Laid, Kenneth C, SINET News, Feb–May 2000

The C-HQLI provide 'the rest of the story' on the USA, its rapidly evolving economy and technological sectors. Statisticians are reformulating GNP to reflect these new realities in re-categorizing software and many other services, which together now represent the largest sector of our 'Information Age' economy. All the world's industrializing societies are undergoing similar changes and restructuring, as they move from the earlier to the later stages of the Industrial Revolution. Part of this great transition is towards information-based economies. Here, knowledge, intellectual capital and the more intangible human and social assets replace manual labour and some of the tangible capital that earlier economic textbooks called the 'factors of production'.

This transition to information-based production and services is often accompanied by a deeper knowledge of natural processes and ecological assets and the services nature provides. Thus, many economies have also evolved towards more efficient use of energy and materials – a shift away from fossil fuels and nuclear power, which create pollution and safety hazards. As we learn more about our living planet and nature's productivity and design genius, our technologies change. They slowly reflect this new knowledge in biotechnologies and the harnessing of clean, inexhaustible sources of energy (from the sun, wind, oceans and biomass). With appropriate full-cost prices and regulations, societies slowly shift to recycling industrial materials in closed-loop production, waste reduction, re-manufacturing and reuse. An industrial design revolution is quietly under way towards more 'weightless', dematerialized economies.

It is well-recognized that macro-economic statistics fell behind in mapping these fundamental shifts. A large part of the problem is that conventional economics and accounting still consider air, water and nature's purifying cycles as being 'free'. Thus, only recently have textbooks begun to embrace full-cost prices. Only in the past decade have we seen the rise of environmental and ecological economics, full-cost accounting and life-cycle costing for investment purposes. All this, together with the rise of social and environmental auditing, accounting for 'intangibles' and intellectual property – and the many attempts to overhaul GNP and GDP – represents the greatest revolution in accounting and statistics since the invention of double-entry bookkeeping. Calvert and this author support the Global Reporting Initiative (GRI) to extend company auditing to measure a triple bottom line.

Economists KW Kapp, Kenneth Boulding, Barbara Ward, EJ Mishan and EF Schumacher in Europe spearheaded these new approaches, as well as Nicholas Georgescu-Roegen and his student Herman Daly, Richard Estes and others in the US. On the conceptual foundations of these early economics innovators, a host of new efforts to redefine human development, wealth and progress emerged in the 1980s and 1990s. David Morris of the Institute for Local Self-Reliance produced the Physical Quality-of-Life Index (PQLI) for the Overseas Development Council; while I promulgated the Country Futures Indicators (CFI) approach in 1986. Herman Daly and John Cobb created the Index of Sustainable Economic Welfare (ISEW) with Clifford Cobb in 1989. This index deducts from GNP many environmental and social costs, arriving at a significantly lower 'net GNP'. This index has been adapted widely in Europe, Australia and the US as the Genuine Progress Index (GPI) since 1995. Other approaches include the Fordham University Index of Social Health devised by Marque Luisa and Marc Miringoff.[6]

The Clinton administration attempted to 'green' the US GDP by means of an Integrated Environmental and Economic Satellite Account (IEESA) developed by the Bureau of Economic Analysis (BEA) of the US Commerce Department in 1994 – to mixed reviews. The Congress directed the BEA to halt this work, and charged the National Research Council to review the entire issue. In late 1999, the Council issued its report, *Nature's Numbers*, urging that the BEA be funded to restart this effort. The World Bank in 1995 issued its own Wealth Index, which redefined 'the wealth of nations' in significant ways. The Bank now defines 60% of this wealth of nations as 'human capital' (social organization, human skills and knowledge), 20% as environmental capital (nature's contribution) and 20% as 'built capital' (factories and finance capital). A revolution has begun in the economics profession, with many of its best minds – Joseph Stiglitz, formerly the World

---

[6] See for example, Challenge, Henderson, H, 'What's New In the Great Debate About Wealth and Progress', ME Sharpe, New York, December 1996

Bank's chief economist, Harvard's Jeffrey Sachs and Paul Krugman – embracing pieces of the new thinking. The most influential, widely used and quoted new formula is the United Nations Human Development Index (HDI), which has spawned many national versions.

The most pressing methodological debate over such new measures of wealth progress and human development has concerned the extent to which such broad new areas of concern as human rights, health, education, environment and overall quality of life can be captured using money coefficients and macro-economic models. Such methods currently weight all data from different economic sectors into one index. Many, including myself, believe that such high levels of aggregating all these 'apples and pears' into one index is inappropriate and often confusing. Another issue concerns the use of 'satellite accounts' for environmental and social data. This designation indicates lesser value for such data. Such diverse areas of quality of life deserve their own metrics – those most appropriate within the diverse disciplines that study such fields. For example, money coefficients cannot quantify human rights, air and water quality, recreational satisfaction, education, health, public safety or national security. Money measures and percentages of national budgets can give clues – but are often simply input data – rather than measuring outcomes and results.

The systems approach used in the C–HQLI requires multiple metrics to cover the 12 aspects of US society. In each area, a model links all major factors and processes, providing a road-map of how decisions flow through various institutional structures to create outcomes. Such systemic models help identify why, in each area, the US has succeeded or fallen short of achieving its stated policy goals. Many Indicator areas show how throwing money at ill-defined problems such as 'crime' or 'national security', or at specific diseases, has led to wasted or misdirected resources, both public and private. These Indicators show how each sector of the US economy contributed to, or in some cases, diminished overall quality of life. The 'holes' in the statistical pictures and where data-gathering needs new focus are identified. These 12 'unbundled' Indicators, with the use of visual models, come together as a broader pattern. This systems approach allows the rigorous display of this wealth of diverse data – without the loss of detail that plagues any single index approach. Each Indicator is summarized below.

1.1 EMPLOYMENT

The field of US employment and work changed immensely during the 1990s. From a recession in the early 1990s, the US in 2000 had the lowest (4.2%) unemployment recorded since the 1950s. This has caused a rethink of the Non-Accelerating Inflation Rate of Unemployment (NAIRU) used by the Federal Reserve Board in setting interest rates. A NAIRU under 5.5% was thought to be inflationary. Until recently the US economy was running at higher levels of employment without this expected rise in inflation – due, many say, to the 'new economy' factors. In spite of the bursting of the bubble on Wall Street, the internet and information technology arguably have raised overall US productivity. The Employment Indicator model also shows that a large but not well-measured percentage of productive work is unpaid. This unpaid work in caring for elders, the sick and children – in home or volunteer organization settings – is unaccounted for in the GNP. Many organizations in the non-profit, civic sector of US society now call for full recognition of the value of this caring work. Some call for housework and parenting to be paid, through statutory pension benefits or in marriage contracts. This area of concern will likely grow as both parents in families are in the paid workforce. The 'family values' debate encodes many new dilemmas faced by parents as they juggle two jobs, child and elder care as the US population ages. World-wide, the United Nations Human Development Index (HDI) in 1995 estimated that unpaid work by the world's women was worth US$11 trillion and that by men another US$5 trillion. This US$16 trillion total was simply missing from the 1995 world GDP of US$24 trillion. In addition, this Indicator tracks the growing ranks of the self-employed, part-timers and the composition by gender, ethnicity and age of the US workforce. The promise of the Industrial Age for more leisure – as machines and automation took over production tasks – did not materialize. Today, Americans work longer hours than their counterparts in Europe and Japan. Yet, there is much debate over the statistics on work and leisure, as cross-referenced in the Indicator on Re-creation.

1.2 INCOME

This Indicator dissects conventional macro-statistics to reveal important information concealed by the averages. Although US incomes at the low end have been essentially flat for over a decade, there were signs of increase due to the 'new economy' phenomenon in 2000. The bear market on Wall Street and softening US economy has, so far, resulted in some increase in unemployment. Yet the gap between rich and poor Americans is still historically high – an issue that does not bode well for any democracy. Other measurement issues include the extent to which technology and globalization are squeezing the incomes of less-skilled Americans and are related to the Employment and Education Indicators. A 1995 national survey by the Merck Foundation and the Harwood Group found that 28% of Americans had opted for lower incomes and moved to rural communities in order to improve their quality of life. Clearly, values are changing and new trade-offs are being made between more income *vis-à-vis* more time, tranquil and less-polluted environments – all made possible by home computers and the internet. As official statistical cameras are re-focused, the Income Indicator will add new data-streams.

1.3 SHELTER

This Indicator dissects US macro-economic data to reveal a 'good news, bad news' picture. The American Dream of home ownership has never been so fulfilled – with a record 66.3% now owning homes. A majority of Americans are well housed with over two-thirds in affordable, physically adequate, uncrowded housing. The bad news is that shelter deprivation still exists in spite of the US economic expansion. Some 5.3 million low-income renters are in distress and an additional half to three-quarters of a million Americans are homeless at any given time. These statistics seem to be a reflection of the national poverty gap – shown in the Income Indicator. The state of shelter in the US also affects opportunities for social mobility and education and thus is related to many other Indicators, including those on Employment, Health and Environment.

1.4 INFRASTRUCTURE

This Indicator unpacks macro-statistics to reveal an ongoing debate: to what extent the US has been overlooking the vital role its infrastructure plays in undergirding its economy. Historically, infrastructure referred to highways, railroads, harbours, bridges, aqueducts, public buildings, dams and the like. Industrial societies evolved airports, communications systems, energy supplies, water and other utilities. Since 11 September 2001, these issues have moved to the centre. Today, infrastructure includes education, research and development, computerized 'backbone' systems and all taxpayer-supported systems used in commerce and on which large sectors of any economy rely.

A recent trend, picked up by this Indicator, is that of the privatization of growing areas of formerly publicly owned infrastructure, including electric utilities, phone, water and other services. After the 2001 electricity black-outs in California, a re-evaluation of deregulation of such vital infrastructure is underway. Such publicly funded investments used to be 'expensed' items in GDP accounts. As of 1996, a more realistic asset budget in GNP now accounts for such investments as 'assets' – since they often have a useful lifetime of 50–100 years or more. This accounting change has contributed to the US budget surplus. Canada changed its GNP to include such public investments as assets in 1999, thereby reducing its deficit by Canadian $50 billion. Japan could much improve its prospects by adopting such budgeting reforms – as could European Union countries. This Indicator is related to most other Indicators, as infrastructure is the key to energy efficiency, whether cities sprawl over virgin lands and farms or whether older or vacant land in our cities is infilled. These factors in turn relate to environmental protection, pollution, housing, education, public health and safety.

1.5 ENERGY

This Indicator is a key to the overall efficiency of an economy. US GNP has been growing with less energy input in the past 25 years, since the first Organization of Petroleum Exporting Countries (OPEC) oil embargo in 1973. But the US still lags behind Japan and Europe – using almost twice the energy they use per unit of GNP. This puts the US in an uncompetitive position and worsens California's electricity crisis – even as the internet-based 'new economy' grows. US reliance on low-fuel-efficiency cars and fossil fuels decreases national flexibility. Entrenched sectors of the older industrial economy oppose the shift to new energy sources, cleaner fuel cell or electric cars. All these issues of restructuring the US economy came to a head in the debate over climate change. The fossil fuel industry lobbied hard and spent millions on advertising campaigns to oppose the 1997 Kyoto Agreements to reduce fossil fuel carbon emissions. Yet the scientific evidence now overwhelmingly points to the need to reduce such emissions. Many analysts, including Amory Lovins of the Rocky Mountain Institute, Colorado, believe that the fossil-industrial transition to the Information Age will usher in a prosperous, profitable economy based on renewable resource use and deeper knowledge. Thus energy efficiency can mean less waste, higher, cleaner profits, more comfortable homes, communities and travel with less pollution. The transition from here to there can be followed in this Indicator, as traditional economic models of 'efficiency' move into alignment with physical realities of thermodynamic efficiency.

1.6 NATIONAL SECURITY

The US public's view of 'national security' has been changing for over a decade, as revealed, for example, in Americans Talk Issues Foundation surveys and those from the University of Maryland's Center on Public Policy Attitudes. Even before the end of the Cold War, the US public was identifying global economic competitiveness and environmental pollution as issues of national security – beyond traditional military views of 'defence'. The National Security Indicator model reveals how Americans, the

Congress, the administration and a host of institutional players actually shape our current national security policy. This identifies other potential lags in the military view of national security. These relate to prevention of threats and conflicts. These must be addressed via intelligence, diplomacy, treaty-making, surveillance and verification – most often involving allies and multilateral agencies including the United Nations (the only global organization of countries that can convene all the parties). Short-changing such anticipatory, preventive policies inevitably leads to more drastic, expensive military interventions – such as those that might have been prevented in Bosnia, Kosovo, East Timor and other trouble-spots. Yet the Indicator shows a growing imbalance between military strategies and programmes against an alarming drop-off in preventive activities – including deteriorating US Embassy facilities, cuts to State Department diplomatic activities, pull-backs from international peacekeeping and surveillance operations with US allies and the United Nations, and the continuing US arrears in paying UN dues. The public debate about a 'new isolationism', the changing meaning of 'national sovereignty' and globalization will continue for years to come – accelerated by the events of 11 September 2001. National security is fundamentally linked to all other areas and Indicators of any nation's quality of life.

1.7 HEALTH

The Health Indicator begins by exploring why the US provides more health-care services at higher costs per capita than any other country in the world. This enormous sector of the economy is becoming a top focus of national concern – since it delivers only modest improvements in health status in some areas and none in others. Since the anthrax incidents, the US public health sector has been revealed as under-funded and woefully inadequate. Almost 50 million Americans have no health insurance and the demand for a 'patient's Bill of Rights' to hold health maintenance organizations (HMOs) and insurance companies more accountable for decisions over patient treatment was supported by both presidential candidates in 2000. The Indicator offers a model of the current US health-care system, which helps to clarify a systemic set of issues. Health is being redefined beyond the medical intervention model. Today, Americans are focusing on prevention, stress-reduction and life-style choices. Tobacco and alcohol use, and even the availability of guns, are issues entering the public health debate. More Americans now consult 'complementary' and 'alternative' health providers than visit conventional medical doctors and facilities. This is a paradigm shift, which is restructuring the entire medical-industrial complex and its technocratic, bureaucratic approach, which represents some 14% of US GNP. New statistics are needed as the US integrates these two very different approaches to health. An October 1999 study in the Federal Reserve Bank of New York's Economic Policy Review cites the effects of urban poverty. Fifteen-year-old black and white males' life expectancy rates were compared in several cities. In poor black areas of New York City only 37% were expected to live to age 65. in Detroit, the figure was 50%. Poor white 15-year-olds in poverty areas of Detroit and Cleveland did a little better: in Detroit, 60% were found likely to live to age 65, with 64% in Cleveland. Average life expectancy for all US whites is 77 years and for US blacks 62 years. The Indicator shows such gaps, which also relate to similar data in the Income, Shelter, Safety, Education and Human Rights Indicators.

1.8 EDUCATION

The Education Indicator model gives an overview of US issues over structural educational reform, school vouchers, 'charter' schools, home schooling and those concerning the shift to today's globalized information-based economy. Knowledge is now widely recognized as a key factor of production. The World Bank and other multilateral institutions now agree that investments in education (particularly at pre-school and kindergarten through 12 levels) are the new key, along with investments in health, to economic development. Statistics, particularly in macro-economic indices, are lagging far behind this new paradigm of economic and human development. Nothing is changing US business and academic institutions faster than the new definitions of capital – as human and intellectual capital.

As many new internet-based e-commerce businesses know, a company cannot 'own' the part of its knowledge base that resides in the heads of its employees. The rise of stock options, partnerships and employee stock ownership plans (ESOPs) are all related to this new evaluation of intellectual capital – on which all technical and social innovation is based. Today, more than ever, education is a basic human right – in many other countries as well as in the US. Furthermore, levels of education will drive all the world's economies towards development – depending on how they structure and invest in educating humanity's most precious resource: the world's children.

1.9 PUBLIC SAFETY

This Indicator maps a rapid evolution in the US debate about this aspect of quality of life. The view that safety was a personal affair and that risk-taking was a private choice has evolved as society became more complex. While individuals are still largely responsible for their behaviour, today we live in an interdependent world. Many risks of daily life (for example, exposure to toxic wastes, gun violence in schools, car and highway design, risks in foods and other products) are involuntary and often unavoidable. Thus the Indicator also captures these new concerns in public safety – and links today's risks to health, education and cultural factors. Crime statistics in the model and the tragedies of US gun violence are seen in this larger setting. This systemic view provides insights for individual and corporate risk-reduction and may help rethink views on improving public safety, and its measurements.

1.10 HUMAN RIGHTS

This Indicator views the state of human rights in the US in broad areas: fundamental rights to the security of person; the US Bill of Rights and Amendments to the Constitution (including freedom of expression, religious freedom, right of assembly and voting rights). The terrorist attacks on the US have led to new legislation giving law enforcement new powers, which are opposed by most civil liberties groups. Beyond these basic rights, the model embraces an evolving international view embodied in the Universal Declaration of Human Rights, which the US signed along with many other countries over 50 years ago. The Indicator covers US incarceration data (among the highest in the world), the death penalty, prison labour, racial/gender discrimination, mistreatment of prisoners and aliens as well as voting rights, participation in politics and the growing influence of money and special interests. Today, human rights have become a keystone of US foreign policy – largely due to the efforts of former President Jimmy Carter. A crucial issue is to what extent the sovereignty of a nation is no longer absolute in cases where despotic dictators violate the human rights of their own citizens. Such clashes were evident in the cases of Bosnia, Kosovo, Rwanda and in the breakaway Russian province of Chechnya. These and other human rights issues are also of great concern in other countries. In Europe, Japan, Canada and many other countries, economic, cultural and social rights (to education, social participation, health care, leisure time and social security) are included. Another evolution concerns the embracing of women and children in the definition of human rights – now widely recognized – if not fully achieved. This Indicator is crucial to quality of life in the US and world-wide.

1.11 ENVIRONMENT

This Indicator seeks to embrace the interactions between human society, economic processes and humanity's life support systems: the natural world, its resources and other species. Naturally, such a task is too enormous to do more than find within the model some key 'surrogate' indicators as proxies for such a vast area. The burgeoning field of environmental indicators and sustainability criteria are drawn upon, including data on planetary ecosystems, the crucial role of biodiversity, human effects on the ozone layer and climate. The Environment Indicator model recognizes these broad concerns, but pays attention to indicators closest to the lives of most US citizens. Air and water quality and attainment of EPA standards are the initial focus, since people cannot survive without acceptable quality air and water. The National Research Council's 1999 report, *Nature's Numbers*, also notes that 'Greater emphasis should be placed on measuring actual human exposures to air and water pollution' (Recommendations 4.3 and 5.9). Through these lenses one can understand better the causes of air and water degradation and pollution – and the many steps needed to reverse these threats. The systems approach reveals that many other domains of quality of life, infrastructure design, energy use, shelter, health, employment, public safety and national security all impinge on the environment and life support systems – for better or worse. EPA's funding will probably be increased, as its expertise was found vital in monitoring anthrax in public buildings and the possible environmental release of pathogens.

1.12 RE-CREATION

This Indicator goes beyond the material aspects of the US and focuses on how Americans use recreation. The Indicator maps extraordinarily diverse forms of recreation in the US – from volunteering in community projects, helping preserve wildlife and serving the poor, to attending concerts museums or enjoying bowling, hunting and fishing. The model traces how the US organizes and spends private and public resources on such recreational activities. The Indicator embraces self-improving experience (from religious and spiritual pursuits to other forms of self-development), patronizing the arts, physical sports and fitness, do-it-yourself, crafts, gardening, home-improvement, hobbies, vicarious experience (TV, video games, internet), socializing and home entertaining, travel and tourism (now the world's biggest industry), even games of chance, betting and chemical escape (alcohol, tobacco and drugs). This Indicator offers a panorama of these evolving activities of US inhabitants, which together form the largest and fastest-growing sector of the US's services-dominated economy. Statistical and methodological debates abound on the size and shape of this emerging 'Attention Economy' (Henderson, 1996) and its implications concerning work and leisure time. The rapid evolution of the entire field of self-development and recreation augurs additional social and political change. Today's drive for self-development – an essentially spiritual need – is now spilling over into US material lives in the growth of socially responsible investments and in communities opting to honour their local past and culture by building museums and art galleries. Over 80 million Americans volunteer at least 5 hours a week to their communities and the non-profit, voluntary sector now stands at 7% of GNP. A poll cited in *Business Week* (1 November 1999) found that 78% of Americans say that they feel the need in their lives to experience spiritual growth – up from 20% in 1994. The Re-creation Indicator will track such changes. As more governments and research groups in the private and civic sectors promulgate such reforms in national accounts and macro-economic statistics, corporations and national policies can be steered towards protecting life support systems and more equitable, transparent and sustainable societies.

The C-HQLI will be continually reviewed, updated and reformulated as US society restructures and evolves. We hope to benefit from expert feedback from the academic community, government agencies and statisticians' new measurements in all of our 12 Indicator domains. The initial responses from all sectors have been favourable and the many comments suggest that the C-HQLI are being used widely as a public information and policy tool – particularly at state and local levels. Our decision not to release any regular media-friendly single number analogs to GDP releases was taken to prevent distortion and maintain a systemic, holistic view. Meanwhile, we continue to present C-HQLI at numerous professional and academic conferences in the USA, Europe, Latin America and Asia, as well as in UNESCO's Encyclopaedia of Life Support Systems.

Respectability For Change

Kaj Embrén, RespectEurope

The Swedish welfare model has its roots in the industrial development period and is based on social contracts between important public players. The model established a win-win situation for society, companies and trade unions and provided a driving force for result-orientated welfare policies that meant a great deal for the daily lives of many people in Sweden. The model was positive for companies and society in general in as much as it meant fewer strikes and provided resources for the community as a whole. National economic objectives were realized through sound economic and employment policies.

Society is now faced with greater challenges, more global than ever before. The greenhouse effect and ethnic and religious conflict in an age of increasing distrust in politicians, companies and the media and where more than half the world's largest economies are not countries but multinational companies. General Motors is bigger than Sweden. Ford is bigger than Spain. Mitsubishi is bigger than Indonesia. CNN and a few other media giants dominate and decide which of the problems should be given most coverage.

Companies that act irresponsibly in the Third World find it difficult to retain their market positions and rapidly lose their financial value. The cost of Shell's involvement in Nigeria is just one example of how things can change and this ominous development will continue. The maths is not at all complicated. You do not need the Nobel Prize to understand that unfair distribution of resources creates new centres of conflict that are costly for both companies and society in general.

This development has created increased awareness and more strategically effective non-governmental organizations (NGOs) that work as stakeholders and co-operate with the media and other stakeholders. Ten years ago there were 20,000 globally active NGOs, today there are more than 41,000. Interplay between trade unions and other NGOs plays an increasingly important role in influencing the market position of companies. One recent example of this is how Friends of The Earth persuaded the multinational power company Balfour Beatty (turnover US$3.2 billion) to withdraw from a large dam project in Ilisu, Turkey.

If this development is so clear, where are the driving forces to unite the general public, companies, politicians, NGOs and the media in overcoming climate change and economic and social injustice? Over-utilization of the world's resources? Lack of democracy and freedom of speech? Can the many new networks we see forming on a global level be the driving force we are looking for? Can market forces ensure that company licence includes triple bottom line accounting? How strong are the driving forces within the UN? What is a legal framework for a new global Corporate Social Responsibility (CSR) contract? What could we learn from a legal international framework such as the Kyoto Protocol?

'Climate change has a twin impact on business. First, companies have to cope with the direct effects of climate change. Second, they may be forced to curb their emissions of greenhouse gases such as carbon dioxide, which are widely held responsible for global warming,' says *Financial Times* journalist Vannesa Houlder. 'We do not believe that there has to be a conflict between business objectives and social and environmental objectives,' says Anders Dahlvig, CEO of Ikea, one of the first companies to integrate The Natural Step – a new way of integrating the social and business objectives of an enterprise – into its business strategy. A growing number of committed companies, NGOs and nations are beginning to find common ground for partnership.

In the wake of the Kyoto Protocol, new initiatives are forming that are also part of a new model for the future. Through RespectTable (a network for CSR actions in Business), Ikea (Denmark/Sweden/Holland), The Body Shop (UK) and Interface Inc (US), energy companies such as Birka (Sweden) and Nuon (Holland) have begun work to increase consumer participation in climate change issues. These companies are driven by a genuine social commitment. Their leadership does not just talk about social ideals but gets involved by doing something to change things.

We are witnessing a more responsible business trend within the private sector, which is often more powerful and progressive than government offices. Companies are becoming more aware of their social responsibility. I know from talking to business executives that they are often asked by their children how they intend to provide for their upbringing and how they intend to solve the threat to the environment and provide them with building blocks for the future. These personal driving forces are necessary if we are to cope with today's social problems. We ourselves, individually or in co-operation with others, must form the building blocks because we can grasp the issues concerning important social problems.

I had the privilege of working with Dr Karl-Henrik Robèrt, the man behind The Natural Step Foundation in Sweden. The Natural Step (TNS) is today an international organization that uses a science-based, systems framework to help organizations, individuals and communities take steps towards sustainability. The mission of TNS is to catalyze systemic change and make fundamental principles of sustainability easier to understand, and meaningful sustainability initiatives easier to implement.

We used the Swedish model of co-operation (consensus) when forming the mission, objectives and methods for The Natural Step. The Natural Step was not only a successful environmental campaign, it was also a new model for joint co-operation over traditional borders – there were NGOs, companies, researchers and public opinion makers. Companies became aware and participated, realized their role in society and changed their business strategies. They acquired a compass and began changing their business strategies step by step.

The Natural Step offered nothing new. It was mainly a pedagogical model for how we as individuals, companies and organizations can utilize the earth's limited resources in a sustainable way. We cannot continue to exhaust our limited resources and poison our environment as we have for the past 200 years. Companies with foresight understood that they would have to restructure their production systems by using natural materials to reduce the dependency on fossil fuels. This would ensure not risking their survival in an ever-competitive market. Not getting involved immediately would cost more in the long term.

Ikea International and Electrolux both realized this at an early stage. The Swedish government was rather put off and found it difficult to handle these positive-minded business executives who discussed topics other than lower taxes and new legislation. These were business executives who discussed economic growth and already had environmental strategies for sustainable development. Traditional industrial lobbyism dissociated itself and could not see its role. Interface, the largest carpet manufacturer in the world, realized at an early stage that they could not continue their industrial production in the same old way. It was one of the first American companies to adopt the philosophy of The Natural Step. The company developed its own CSR programme as a natural part of its business strategy. They no longer sell their products but lease them on a return basis. They take responsibility for the entire production chain and adapt to the laws of nature. The common denominators for many of the pioneer companies that have adapted their manufacturing procedures to the laws of nature is that they have systematically questioned products, services and human behaviour and have leaders with motivating powers, who know how to bring out the best in their workforce.

More and more sectors of society are beginning to realize that they have to reorganize and adapt. The financial sector has been taken by surprise over how new thinking has taken off but has responded with ethical placement codes, the Dow Jones Sustainability Index and SRI (Socially Responsible Investing) funds. The growth of SRI funds is steadily increasing and showing a better earnings yield than traditional investments. According to S&P Micropol, the UK Ethical Funds have enjoyed an increase in returns of between 40%–80% since 1996.

Driving forces now tend to reward long-term investments. We can only hope that economic courses at universities and colleges also start to teach triple bottom line accounting. The market practices of consumers and, in some cases, even institutional investors have begun to show a change of strategy. Ten per cent is usually enough seriously to alter the pace of change. We are closing in on that limit, which is my starting point for establishing the basis of a new social contract that will concern us all. A social contract must involve both global and local perspectives. It must be systematic and long term.

Democratic freedom of speech and participation are also important parts of the model, which meets all the requirements for becoming accepted among the general public, companies, politicians and the media.

One of my main points is that The Natural Step can contribute to a more systematic approach to the problems we face. It is based on the laws of nature and the smallest building blocks of our life, our cells. Our cells do not discuss politics or economics; they only require the right conditions to continue living and developing. As a society we are systematically altering the ecosystem structures and functions that provide life-supporting services for us all.

The Natural Step four system conditions are:

1. CONCENTRATIONS OF SUBSTANCES EXTRACTED FROM THE EARTH'S CRUST

In a sustainable society, human activities such as the burning of fossil fuels and the mining of metals and minerals will not occur at a rate that causes them systematically to increase in the ecosphere. There are thresholds beyond which living organisms and ecosystems are adversely affected by increases in substances from the earth's crust. Problems may include an increase in greenhouse gases leading to global warming, contamination of surface and ground water, and metal toxicity which can cause functional disturbances in animals. In practical terms, this means substituting certain minerals that are scarce in nature with others that are more abundant, using all mined materials efficiently and systematically reducing dependence on fossil fuels.

COMMENTS:

Phasing out fossil fuels from our productive apparatus will take time, and we must find ways to do it. We will find the basis for alternative development by systematically asking how we can reduce oil production. Even the oil companies have realized this and have started to call themselves energy companies. Who would have thought ten years ago that BP and Shell would be investing US$500 million each over the next three years in green energy projects? That is more than the total annual Swedish environmental budget (US$300 million).

2. CONCENTRATIONS OF SUBSTANCES PRODUCED BY SOCIETY

In a sustainable society, humans will avoid generating systematic increases in persistent substances such as DDT, PCBs and freon. Synthetic organic compounds such as DDT and PCBs can remain in the environment for many years, bio-accumulating in the tissue of organisms, causing profound deleterious effects on predators in the upper levels of the food chain. Freon, and other ozone depleting compounds, may increase the risk of cancer due to added UV radiation in the troposphere.

This means systematically substituting certain persistent and unnatural compounds with ones that are normally abundant or break down more easily in nature, and using all substances produced by society efficiently.

COMMENTS:

We must increase our knowledge of unnatural compounds and begin developing new materials. Investors will queue up to finance material for sustainable development.

3. IMPOVERISHED BY PHYSICAL DISPLACEMENT, OVER-HARVESTING OR OTHER FORMS OF ECOSYSTEM MANIPULATION

In a sustainable society, humans will avoid taking more from the biosphere than can be replenished by natural systems. In addition, people will avoid systematically encroaching upon nature by destroying the habitat of other species. Biodiversity, which includes the great variety of animals and plants found in nature, provides the foundation for ecosystem services that are necessary to sustain life on this planet. Society's health and prosperity depends on the enduring capacity of nature to renew itself and rebuild waste into resources. This means drawing resources only from well-managed ecosystems, systematically pursuing the most productive and efficient use of these resources and of land, and exercising caution in all modification of nature.

COMMENTS:

The Amazon rainforest is still being damaged by reckless felling, it is just that CNN is not reporting it. Ten years ago it made the headlines, today, despite illegal felling being more widespread than it was then, it only warrants a paragraph. Over-fishing is another serious problem. Industrial vacuum cleaning of the sea-bed has no realistic link with the laws of nature, but this phenomenon continues throughout the world.

Consumers are beginning to ask where the fish or the outdoor furniture comes from. This is the beginning of a consumer activism that helps many people to think again.

An international environmental tribunal is said to be the next step to counteract this development.

4. RESOURCES ARE USED FAIRLY AND EFFICIENTLY IN ORDER TO MEET HUMAN NEEDS GLOBALLY

Considering human enterprise as a whole, we need to be efficient regarding the use of resources and waste generation in order to be sustainable. If one billion people lack adequate nutrition while another billion have more than they need, there is a lack of fairness with regard to meeting basic human needs. Achieving greater fairness is essential for social stability and the co-operation needed for making large-scale changes within the framework as laid out by the first three conditions.

To achieve this fourth condition, humanity must strive to improve technical and organizational efficiency around the world and to live using fewer resources, especially in affluent areas. System condition four implies an improved means of addressing human population growth. If the total resource throughput of the global human population continues to increase, it will be increasingly difficult to meet basic human needs as human-driven processes intended to fulfil human needs and wants are systematically degrading the collective capacity of the Earth's ecosystems to meet these demands. This means using all of our resources efficiently, fairly and responsibly so that the needs of all people on whom we have an impact, and the future needs of people who are not yet born, stand the best chance of being met.

IN PRACTICE:

The Body Shop and Greenpeace are involved in an international campaign called Positive Energy that focuses on the fact that two billion people lack renewable energy. When companies and NGOs start to co-operate it creates a driving force because both have something to gain. This model provides the basis for a new social model. A social contract that involves important social aspects and facilitates effective decision-making and accomplishment.

THE NEW SOCIAL CONTRACTS

The new social and environmental sustainable contracts will probably be formed with the help of new networks and develop as voluntary agreements. The systematic building blocks developed by The Natural Step are part of the new driving force that will help global society face the challenges ahead.

We should also learn from the Swedish welfare models of the 1940s, 1950s and 1960s. The Swedish welfare model cannot serve as an actual guide for a new social contract. But, it is an interesting study for the interplay and consensus between companies, politicians, organizations and the general public, which is achieved without the various groups losing their group identity.

Experience also shows that accountability must be included in all social systems that will involve companies, authorities, politicians, NGOs and the media. Those who cannot manage to analyze critically their model, programme, story or concept through independent resources have no future.

Activating Shareholders

Robert AG Monks

I want to take you on a bit of a trip. It's a visual trip. There's been a lot of talk about shareholder activism of various kinds, and the importance of putting it into context. The context has been provided by the title of this book – *Enterprising Europe*. To understand shareholder activism thoroughly, we must first identify the shareholders and also identify what can be done to encourage greater activism and shareholder accountability. I will argue that this is the responsibility of the government; much in the way the UK is doing by implementing the Myners' report on improving existing law, which encourages activism in theory but makes it virtually impossible for institutional shareholders to act.

The first thing that you have to do when you have a trust is to understand that you have to administer the trust for the interest of somebody, and I'm going to say who that somebody is. I will explore the entire universe of institutional investors, who are the trustees. I will then discuss beneficial laws, government failure and finally a few companies who I think are doing, or are beginning to do, things that are worth our support. In all of these themes I will be bringing you both some good news and some bad news.

When you hear that it is the legal obligation of fiduciaries to run a corporation for the benefit of the shareholders, why did no one ever stop to think that there are all kinds of different people called shareholders? And that they have very, very different interests. When the identity of the shareholders is vague, our efforts to increase trustee accountability to shareholders is blunted because we can't specifically identify for whom the trust exists and thereby create a set of standards that need to be enforced.

Think of a tree. It's sacred to the Hindus, it means life. If you look at the tree as a representation of shareholders, at the top are the arbitrageurs. They own the stock. Do we run the company for their benefit? They own the stock for ten seconds, ten micro-seconds. Program managers – the computer – decide what stocks they own. Do we run the corporation for them? Sometimes they're in and out of stocks in a week, in a month, in a year. Mutual funds – they have stock ownership that relates to the tax problems of their beneficiaries. Bank trustees – they're a little more conservative, and they hold stock for a longer time. Insurance companies have to collateralize long-term liability – pension funds. And then finally, of course, the root is index funds. It means for many, owning a lot of stock forever. Who is the shareholder? The interests of the arbitrageurs, the first group, are not at all the interests of the index fund holder. So, if you are going to have a meaningful notion of a fiduciary responsibility you have to understand who is the person for whom you are running it. And I suggest that the defined benefit plan holder is the appropriate shareholder.

Pension fund beneficiaries typically have 18 years to go before retirement and represent a huge percentage of the total population. These plan participants, interested in retirement in the years ahead, want to retire into a clean, safe and civil world. So, you can begin to see that you can define the scope of the obligation you owe as a trustee to the defined benefit pension plan holder.

Turning from the beneficiary of the trust, it is important to consider the extraordinary expansion in the last 50 years in the world of institutional investment. The size of the total outstanding equity in the US in 1999 was almost US$19 trillion, with institutional owners holding US$9 trillion and representing approximately 50%. My book, *New Global Investors*, describes this development in detail.

An entirely new world has been created. We used to have a world of business. We now have a business world and a world of ownership of business. And the world of ownership of business is much more profitable than the world of business. This is one of the problems. Managing money and providing ancillary services is probably the most profitable business in the history of the world. This has created a good news/bad news situation – creating a lot of revenue with which good things can be done, but making it very difficult to change things because so many people have such a large vested interest in keeping things the way they are. Institutional holders in the United States alone hold US$9 trillion in assets. In the UK the institutions own a larger percentage of publicly held company stock than in any other country in the world. Only long-term shareholders have the perspective and the interest to assure congruency of ownership and societal values.

There is good news. According to UK Chancellor of the Exchequer Gordon Brown, UK fiduciaries who fail to take an activist stance because of a wider business interest would be illegitimately subordinating the interest of their clients. In other words, if the trustee fails to be activist because of fear of scaring off future clients, the trustee can be held liable for not acting in the best interests of the beneficiaries. Brown's initiatives may well be the beginning of something being done about this problem in the rest of the English-speaking world.

Paul Myners' report (which, of course, is the basis of the Chancellor's recommendations) also says, 'Just because you do good for other people doesn't mean you shouldn't do good'. Makes sense to me. Let me go back to the private pension funds. This is by far the largest category of institutional owners. This is the private company pension fund, like Shell, BP and British Tobacco. If you look at what is supposed to be the Golden Rule – and it comes straight from self-interest – it is the management of company 'X' saying: 'Our pension fund will treat your management the way your pension fund treats our management.'

And the management of company 'X' appoints the trustee of the employee benefits plan. They could have appointed some bank to be the trustee. Now we are talking, in the American context, of about a US$5 trillion pension fund. Well, by and large if you picked up half a per cent of the management fee, that's US$25 billion. Then add to that the control over the brokerage commission, which is another half of one per cent, or

US$25 billion. This is an immensely profitable business – perhaps more in the City of London than in the United States.

So, the trustee of the employee benefit plan hires investment managers. Trustees are in a very difficult position. The trustee, when paid at all, is paid very little and is dealing with people who are rich beyond belief, as a result of decisions that they made. It is a very difficult situation. The investment managers of the equity portfolio own stock in company 'Y' and company 'Z'. What I am urging is that the investment manager be an activist about company 'Y' and company 'Z'. The investment manager who is getting some portion of this 50 billion dollars from company 'X' is faced with the Golden Rule problem: if he is active, he will make the trustees of company 'Y' and company 'Z' pension fund very upset with him. They may retaliate with company 'X' or, even worse, they may retaliate by not having the investment manager on the shortlist of people who can get the next pension fund.

Institutional money management is one of the biggest industries in the world. The amount of money is simply staggering in terms of its impact on whole communities. The profit margins are the highest in the world and yet it is subject to this circular system, in which so much money is involved that people are virtually inhibited from doing their plain legal duty.

Now – the foundations and the universities. I have been appalled, in the case of universities that I have personally been affiliated with, that they simply will not undertake responsibility as owners of the securities in their portfolios, even as they offer world famous tuition in ethics and philosophy. The same thing is true of the great foundations. These are people who our society considers leaders. And yet we have tolerated a system in which they don't act and they do not require their money managers to act. The problem is outlined in a letter that I received from one of my closest personal friends, a former chief executive officer of a major international fiduciary bank. His position was that he could not be an activist because his customers didn't like it. He is the most honourable man I know. And when he made his point, I had great empathy with him. He was someone who wanted to do the right thing, would do it, but was aware the system prevented him from doing it because if he was activist his customers would go to another bank. And so as long as you have uneven law enforcement, people like him, who absolutely want to do the right thing, can't do it because to do so is to create risk for the people who work for them. And so this is a place where we need the law to be enforced.

The law is very clear. The trustees are obligated to run the trust for the benefit of the beneficiaries who, I would suggest, are the equivalent of the long-term pension plan owners. Universities are ignoring the law. So are foundations and private corporations. And the government created this problem. It used to be when you talked about owners of companies you were talking about a roster of rich people and a faceless public. Nowadays, you have institutions, largely pension funds. And the institutions own so much of the stock that the opportunity for flesh and blood people to have any real role is gone. The institution was created as an unintended consequence of retirement and savings policy, and because the government won't enforce the law, institutions don't have to follow it.

Respective ownership involvement in corporate governance will not be possible until and unless the government effectively corrects the problem that it has created. Even the most doctrinaire lover of small government would have to agree that you want the government to undo the mess that it has made. So, I make no apology in saying that the government has to do something here. They've got to cut the road-block. They either have to enforce this law that says that trustees must be active, or they have to provide some other way for corporate governance to operate. All of the fiduciary laws – those covering investment trusts, charities, pension funds and banks trusts – must be the same. It has to be the same law. The government in the UK has now said: 'Once and for all we think it is important to have an empowered owner.' This must be effectively implemented and enforced.

Let me go back to the values of the beneficiary. I have already mentioned the reasons why the pensioner is the appropriate beneficiary of all these trusts, long term. The person for whom a trustee runs a corporation is long term. Let there be no doubt about that. They run it for people who are not inanimate objects, but instead human beings, who want to retire into a civil society. They want companies to follow policies that will make it a clean world and a civil society. And so, never again let anybody be confused about who is the shareholder of a corporation. We have a law with all kinds of wonderful provisions that nobody can enforce. The theoretical ability of shareholders to run a corporation has been impeded by often well-intended laws, the result of which has been to bring us to a total stop. We are now ready to move on.

It will require much experience, many mistakes, patience and perseverance for a detailed ownership agenda to be articulated. But we can make a start. All institutions should require that the companies in which they invest adopt the following policies:

- Disclose publicly how their functioning impacts society
- Obey the law
- Exercise restraint in influencing and financing government.

If these policies are faithfully observed, the public can have confidence that it lives in a country with laws that legitimately express the will of the people, and it can be content simply to require corporations to behave lawfully.

Triple Bottom Line Strategies, Stakeholder Engagement And Corporate Reporting

John Elkington, SustainAbility

Sustainable development is on the political and business agendas but remains diffuse for many people. The 'triple bottom line' (TBL) language was developed as a way of helping business people to boil down the complexity – and to see immediate action points in terms of accounting, auditing, reporting and the management systems needed for these processes to deliver improved performance. SustainAbility's thinking on this agenda has been outlined in two books and a series of reports.

The TBL agenda is being driven by a range of factors, including: (1) growing concerns about issues like globalization, human rights and climate change; (2) the related pressures on companies and such institutions as the G8, IMF and WTO; (3) the growing professionalization of the area, through the activities of eg standard-setters, accountants and auditors; (4) the growing interest of financial markets, as illustrated by such indices as the Dow Jones Sustainability Group Indices and the FTSE4Good Index; and (5), in response to such trends, the use of TBL-related positionings and initiatives as part of corporate strategies designed to build competitive advantage.

SUCCESSFUL SOLUTIONS AND STRATEGIES

The most obvious solutions often have to do with technology (eg renewable energy, fuel cells). But key challenges relate to markets, corporate cultures and organizational learning. In terms of the cultural dimensions, the challenge is shifting from internalizing TBL externalities and including new stakeholders to that of integrating thinking, priorities, targets and action right across the agenda. Values are increasingly central, which is why the term 'values added' is increasingly heard.

Given that many companies and institutions operate their economic, social and environmental activities in departmental silos, there is a growing integration challenge. This is a key reason why the sustainability agenda increasingly cuts across the global and corporate governance agendas, and why CEOs and boards are increasingly involved.

SustainAbility's forward plan:

- Business case: we need to develop the business case, both for business and governments. This is a programme for the United Nations Environment Programme (UNEP) exploring the business case for sustainable development, with parallel projects working with companies and the International Finance Corporation (looking at the business case from a developing world perspective). Report: *Buried Treasure: uncovering the business case for corporate sustainability.*
- Chrysalis: we must work out how to drive market and corporate metamorphosis. This programme focuses on market and corporate transformation. First publication: *The Chrysalis Economy.*
- Emerging markets: with the bulk of global population growth likely to happen in the developing world, we need to look at the future through a different set of lenses. This programme focuses on the developing world agenda, with ongoing projects with eg Ford Motor Company in India.
- Engaging stakeholders: transparency, reporting and bench-marking are key drivers of change. This research programme started in 1994, with UNEP as our long-term partner and with support from over 20 international companies. The focus has been on corporate environmental (and now sustainability) reporting. First international bench-mark reporting, *The Global Reporters*, published 2000. Latest report: *Driving Sustainability* which focuses on the auto sector.
- Janus: corporate lobbying rarely helps drive sustainable development. This programme, developed with GPC – a leading firm of lobbyists –

focuses on today's corporate lobbying and explores ways of building multi-interest lobbies for positive change. First report: *Politics and Persuasion: corporate influence on sustainable development policy*.

- Media: the CNN world provides the matrix within which the TBL agenda will evolve. This international sector study for UNEP focuses on the coverage of sustainable development by the media, in the context of emerging media business models, technologies and ownership patterns.
- Trimaran: where does (and should) the buck stop? This joint programme with the International Business Leaders Programme focuses on corporate governance and the changing role of boards. Latest publication: *The Power to Change: mobilizing board leadership to deliver sustainable value to markets and society*.

To implement an enterprise strategy for Europe, we need to:

- Link the sustainability agenda to positive trends in enterprise, technology, competitive advantage, wealth creation and employment.
- Win the support of business leaders and the financial markets they obey. One possibility: briefings on the strategy – and its market implications – for all major socially responsible investment funds.
- Organize a regular series of events to review progress, ideally as part of existing mainstream initiatives, eg the World Economic Forum summits in Davos.

Accountability Matters

John Sabapathy, Tanya Schwarz and Simon Zadek,
Institute of Social and Ethical Accountability

Accountability: to be accountable for something is to explain or justify the acts and omissions for which one is responsible to people with a legitimate interest. Acountability must also incorporate an understanding of how organizations can learn from accountability processes to improve wider aspects of performance.

In a globalized world, we are linked to ever more people at both personal and professional levels. This interlinking strengthens our social networks; at the same time it extends further our personal and institutional responsibilities, and thereby our accountability.

Our mission at the Institute of Social and Ethical Accountability (AccountAbility) is to develop processes and practices that guide and support the efforts of private, public and voluntary organizations to be transparent and responsive to stakeholders within a performance driven context. The process of delivering accountability to stakeholders actually unlocks entrepreneurialism by providing organizations with access to stakeholder perspectives not often seen and by strengthening the organization's capacity to derive valuable knowledge from such new sources in new ways.

There is still much to learn about the 'how?' and the 'so what?' of accountability. A central question we face today is, how can accountability and the values it embodies be harnessed to contribute to entrepreneurial energy in all sectors, so that today's entrepreneurs can create true wealth?

Conversely, how can entrepreneurial energy infuse the rationale and practice of accountability?

Within an entrepreneurial context there are a number of priorities, which are simultaneously needs, challenges and opportunities:

1. We need to support entrepreneurial learning among organizations that are engaging with their stakeholders. Making oneself accountable strengthens the organization, providing it with new business insights, relationships, strategies and market opportunities. At the same time the core goal of accountability to stakeholders should not be displaced.
2. Accountability processes and stakeholder engagement activity must be extended beyond the core group of leading companies in Europe that have driven the process historically. Without external acknowledgement of the value of accountability, leaders may become isolated and motivation will decline.
3. The investment community should be targeted as a key influence in the market. The value that investors can place via accountability on key issues such as governance, risk and business development is high. Strategies in this area should be prioritized.
4. We need to reward companies that are leading in terms of transparency and social responsibility. Recognition should come at a number of levels; governmental, market, peer-to-peer and media.
5. Strategies that promote accountability and energize companies need to be adapted to support small and medium-sized enterprises (SMEs).

Strategies are many and varied. The following examples of implementation strategies, which correspond to the priorities outlined above, introduce AccountAbility's approach to the challenges ahead.

The revised version of the AA1000 Process Standard, launched in 2000, will place learning and innovation at the core of accountability – ensuring that improvements in performance are aligned to improvements in accountability.

AccountAbility is actively promoting the accountability agenda globally.

Leading by example and argument should be used to drive leading practice and learning further into the mainstream. Key targets include professional training bodies, business schools and consulting firms.

AccountAbility is seeking to strengthen governance and risk management issues within the revised AA1000. Projects such as Gradient, a rating system for assessing companies' performance on labour issues in supply chains, are engaging with key socially responsible investment advocates.

We have initiated Gradient, which will allow greater recognition of good practice on labour issues to be rewarded, while also acknowledging challenges and limitations in extending such practices.

The revised AA1000 standard is being devised to create supportive frameworks for SMEs.

The connections to other areas of the enterprise strategy are many and interrelated. Accountability runs through all areas insofar as it encourages transparency and on-going learning in all processes and organizations.

Key areas to understand include: How can innovation be generated and supported through *accountability* and *Corporate Social Responsibility* activities? What are the useful *indicators, accounts and metrics* associated with this that can aid rather than obstruct decision-making? How do such metrics underpin *ethical funds* and how can ethical funds be mainstreamed? What is the potential impact on *new corporate structures* from a 'stakeholder' model of engagement and accountability?

In implementing any enterprise strategy there are three specific recommendations.

1. The implementation should focus on the strategy's relevance at different functional levels within a business. For example, how can board directors, risk managers and heads of R&D actually implement the enterprise strategy in their day to day work?
2. Communication via business schools should be encouraged, both academic and corporate, in order to raise awareness within existing and future business advocates.
3. Processes and practices supporting organizational accountability must

clearly incorporate effective ways for the organization to identify and learn what aspects of performance it can improve as a result of engaging with its stakeholders.

Education And Enterprise Success

Professor Tom Cannon, RespectLondon

JUST HARDCORE

The overall theme of this book is the creation of a European enterprise strategy. At the heart of this strategy for Europe must be a willingness to challenge the myths and misunderstandings that have emerged about the nature and origins of entrepreneurial success.

The first is the importance in the mythology of entrepreneurship of the notion of the self-made man or woman. The literature is full of descriptions by entrepreneurs themselves of their alienation from traditional educational processes. One of today's most prominent entrepreneurs – Richard Branson – expresses his view that he:

'Felt, like all kids do, that the education we were having stuffed down our throats was quite inappropriate to what we were interested in and what was useful as far as the outside world was concerned.'

Over a hundred years earlier Carnegie came at the issue from a different direction, but reached a similar conclusion. He argued that those without the advantages of education had an edge when competing in the rough and tumble of the entrepreneurial market-place:

'Look out for some boys poorer, much poorer than yourselves, whose parents cannot afford to give them the advantages of a course in this institute, advantages which *should* give you a decided lead in the race – look out that such boys do not challenge you at the post and pass you at the grandstand. Look out for the boy who has to plunge into work direct from the common school and who begins by sweeping out the office.'

This world-view has many attractions for independence-seeking entrepreneurs. They have, in effect, won their way on their own efforts and owe little to the wider community.

Second, this view has much appeal to wider society. It creates a distance between, for example, the world of education and the world of commerce, or at least those sectors of the world of commerce linked with entrepreneurial achievement. For many European policy-makers and writers on education this appealed to both their world view and their beliefs about the purpose of education. Stephen Fry's comment that: ' … The competitive spirit is an ethos, which it is the business of universities such as the one in which I have the honour to move and work to subdue and neutralize … ' echoes down 200 years of educational writing from Chesterton to Arnold, through Hardy and Bennett.

Rejecting thoughts of a positive link between entrepreneurship and education fits well with the self-image of the entrepreneurs and the wishes of many in education.

It is, however, clear that the empirical evidence on the links between entrepreneurship does not support these assumptions or aspirations. Longitudinal studies of entrepreneurship suggests that there is a link between education and entrepreneurship. This exists on several levels. There is, for example, the powerful link between technological change – often emerging from universities – and rates of business formation. Shane argues that[1] :

'Technological change enhances new venture formation by creating

[1] Shane, S, 'Explaining variation in rates of entrepreneurship in the United States: 1899-1988', *Journal of Management*, Sep–Oct 1996, v22 n5 (35)

new opportunities for combining resources in new ways to create new production functions. In addition, empirical evidence has also been gathered which supports this view. Blau (1987) has shown that changes in technology are associated with changes in the rate of self-employment in the US; Brittain and Freeman (1980) have shown that new organizational formation is influenced by technological change.'

This link is borne out by Shane's research into the lead factors in new firm formation. His research shows that:

'Rates of entrepreneurship change over time in a non-random manner. These changes appear to be a function of the rate of technological change.'

Technological change is, for example, more important in determining the rate at which people seek to and succeed in creating new business than, for instance, interest rates.

There is a link, albeit weaker, between new business formation and survival rates and educational attainment levels.

'Education is positively associated with the tendency to be an entrepreneur possibly because the entrepreneur may find a higher rate of return on his or her educational investment when self employed than could be obtained as an employee.'[2]

Other studies have found that this tendency is stronger among women than among men. There is, also, evidence that new firm formation tends to occur in places where there are colleges and universities. This prompted Stinchcombe[3] to conclude that:

---

[2] Shane, *ibid*
[3] Stinchcombe, A, 'Organizations and social structure', pp. 142-193 in March, J (Ed.), *Handbook of Organizations*, Chicago, Rand McNally, 1965

'Literacy and schooling raise practically every variable which encourages the formation of organizations and the staying power of new organizations.'

Dramatic support for this notion of staying power was provided by Dolinsky *et al*'s[4] analysis of the effects of education on the survival, as entrepreneurs, of people with different levels of educational achievement. They found that:

'The incidence of self employment, as measured by the percent of total person years spent in self employment, increases dramatically with increasing levels of educational achievement. It increases from a total of 2.3% for the least well educated to 3.7% for high school only graduates to 5.7% for those with some college or higher education.'

AN OPTIONAL EXTRA?

In this environment, education for enterprise or entrepreneurship is not an optional extra but a central plank in the search for industrial competitiveness and widening economic opportunities. In current government parlance, it ought to be the point at which, in Britain, competitiveness strategies and 'The New Deal' come together, or across Europe, enterprise and social and employment issues merge.

High rates of participation in further and higher education (HE) would seem to provide the gateway into new opportunities for graduates and new routes to competitiveness for the community. The UK's historically low rates of participation would appear to be a barrier to success. The most dynamic countries – in terms of new business formation and/or growth – have much higher rates of educational participation.

There is some evidence that rates of new business formation among graduates are linked with:

● Subjects – with engineering-related and business-related subjects more

---

[4] Dolinsky, AL, Caputo, RK, and Pasumarty, QH, 'The effects of education on business ownership', *Entrepreneurship; theory and practice*, Fall, 1993

likely to stimulate early, successful and, where necessary, repeat start-ups than science, the arts and humanities.

- Mentors and models – institutions that have structures for mentoring graduate starters or where there are models for success are more likely to produce high rates of business formation.
- Clustering – when clusters of strong, externally active HE institutions exist there is likely to be a high rate of new business formation by locals (from within the academic community) and high rates of inward migration by prospective entrepreneurs.
- Finance – availability of local finance for 'academic enterprises' is closely associated with success in the Bay area of San Francisco, Boston and Cambridge (England).

In sum, a Europe seeking to stimulate strong, high-added-value new or growing businesses seems to need high levels of participation in supportive HE institutions. Early creation of new business by those leaving HE is likely to be a minority activity for the foreseeable future. This highlights the problems of education for enterprise for those currently working in different types of enterprise.

Those entrepreneurs and their host communities that get to the future first have some common features. They do not rely on convention. They see that conventional thinking is centred on the past and usually reflects the capabilities of currently dominant organizations.

There is evidence that high-growth organizations keep their eyes on enabling knowledge. They recognize the importance of enabling technologies in creating opportunities for extensive business development.

The most successful concerns wed an entrepreneurial approach to the ability to spot large business gaps and deploy the resources to exploit these opportunities. Incremental developments have less value in revolutionary change. The fluidity of the environment places a premium on the ability of managers and leaders to lead, wheel and deal, and in the process redefine the environment to maximize their opportunities. The sharp increase in competitiveness at times of rapid change calls for an increase in competitive drive across the enterprise.

The central irony of this type of change lies in the need to innovate and change with little knowledge of likely outcomes. We must act now but we do not know the likely result of our actions; however, that is the central paradox of entrepreneurial behaviour.

Making Corporate Social Responsibility Work

What follows are five contributions from people and organizations actively engaged in the development, promotion and delivery of Corporate Social Responsibility (CSR) initiatives

Europe, enterprise and society

Andrew Wilson, Ashridge Centre for Business and Society, UK

The role of business in society has never been so widely discussed. Much of the current debate centres on the notion that the authority of government has been diluted in the face of increasing corporate power. Against this background, discussion about the development of Corporate Social Responsibility (CSR) has tended to polarize around the relative status of business and government. What has so far been under-played is the huge potential for business and government to work together to address some of the most pressing issues facing society today. Partnership initiatives between the two sectors have the potential to make a substantial difference to the social and economic performance of a country. This belief has a number of common underpinnings. Principal among these is agreement that the nature and scale of the social challenges means that governments cannot tackle them alone.

Against this background, European governments are beginning to define a new role – both for themselves and their business partners. Coming to terms with this changing role, and developing constructive partnerships, represents a challenge for both business and government. To portray this as simply the retreat of the state against the onslaught of big business is to misinterpret an important development in the CSR debate. Governments can no longer claim that they have little influence on the development of CSR. By seeking to develop partnerships with business for social welfare provision – at home and abroad – governments across Europe have raised the stakes. What is needed is a careful and considered exploration of the extent of governmental responsibility and, by implication, the limits of CSR.

- All actors in society need to contribute to the development of a new model of business success that properly encompasses the broader social role of companies.
- National governments need to articulate clearly their expectations and requirements of business in delivering CSR initiatives – both as individual actors and in partnership with government.
- There needs to be the creation of mechanisms for dialogue between government, business and civil society to ensure that partnership initiatives deliver societal goals rather than market orientated or governmental driven 'solutions'.
- Partnership working requires different skills and competencies. Paramount is a more inclusive approach to management and leadership. Finding and developing people with the right type of mind-set to operate in this new environment is critical.
- All actors in society need to view capitalism as an ecology like any other, subject to the same principles of interdependence and sustainability as any natural ecological system.
- There is a need for new networks to encourage active collaboration between the separate fragments of business, government and civil society.
- All organizations – business, government and non-governmental organizations (NGOs) – should be encouraged to articulate clearly the values that underpin their activities and the principles by which they are implemented.
- All organizations should be encouraged to report on their performance against their values and principles – in terms of economic, social and environmental impacts.

- Business education at all levels (from school to executive education) should seek to develop tomorrow's leaders in government, business and civil society who have the ability to understand the broader social and environmental implications of the decisions taken by their organizations.

Ashridge is currently working with a number of organizations in both the public and private sector to help them ensure that their values and principles are fully integrated into their strategic decision-making processes. In several instances the aim is to help companies realize attractive returns to investors and achieve broader social objectives.

In July 2001, Ashridge launched the Sir Christopher Harding Leadership Programme – sponsored by British Nuclear Fuels, British Telecom, Consignia and United Utilities. This initiative draws together aspiring leaders from business, government and the voluntary sector. The programme provides a mix of leadership development, skills building, and the opportunity to make a difference by working on a consultancy assignment with organizations whose objective is to bring about positive social change. Currently, participants are helping organizations in such areas as tackling homelessness and finding employment opportunities for ex-offenders.

This issue appears to be central to the main thrust of the European enterprise strategy initiative. At its heart lies the simple question of defining the limit of corporate social responsibilities. What role does business have in bridging the gap between the haves and the have-nots? How is this role played-out in conjunction with national governments and other actors in society? The answers to these questions imply the development of networks, collaborations and partnerships to address the most pressing issues of social justice and social welfare.

- The European enterprise strategy should assist and encourage existing initiatives in this field, such as the joint CSR Europe/TCC European working group which aims to establish a CSR Academy supported by a number of European business schools.
- The European Commission should support proposals set out in the recent Green Paper on CSR by funding a dedicated programme of research that

examines the interface between corporate and governmental social responsibility.

Further investigation is required into the effectiveness and efficiency of partnership working between business and government. Specifically, the goal should be to examine the social impact of such partnerships relative to initiatives that might be taken by one sector acting alone.

Finance and Human Resource Management (HRM) are the main driving forces of CSR

Robert Rubinstein, Brooklyn Bridge

The most important offshoot of CSR seed germination has been its symbiotic fertilization by the forces of human resource management (HRM) and finance (company profit and valuation). One sees clearly business's holism and interconnection by following short-term, single focus policy and its effects and comparing it to long-term, all encompassing values. Finding, keeping and inspiring employees has reached epic importance, with vast industries feeling HRM's insatiable thirst. On the financial side, the 'valuation' of a company has become a full-time effort by investor relations with enormous access to the board of directors. In some cases, they are on the board itself. An expected result of both finance and HRM flourishing in a healthy environment is that they are forcing companies to embrace CSR or 'values leadership'.

Tracing its historical roots back to the American Quakers in the 17th century, who refused to profit from war and slavery, Socially Responsible Investing (SRI) has grown dramatically in the last decade throughout the world. Present-day SRI funds have widened the scope by refusing to profit from the following[1]:

- War industry
- Environmental pollution
- South African apartheid

---

[1] *Investing for Good: making money while being socially responsible*, Kinder, Peter, Lyndenberg, Steven D, Domini, Amy L, Harper Business

- Inferior treatment of minorities and women
- Human Rights abuses
- Poor community relations
- Sub-standard product quality
- Nuclear power
- Alcohol, tobacco or gambling.

The Quakers found war and slavery reprehensible and operated from a strong moral and ethical conviction. This idea of effecting societal change through business and investment has gone through many historical landmarks[2]. The Age of Reform (1890–1917) in the Untied States was a major influence on the consciousness of CSR, during which the Social Creed of the Churches (4 December 1908) laid out what was felt that a society must achieve in the way of social justice. This carried on slowly until picking up steam during the American Civil Rights movement and the Vietnam War. Starting in the watershed year of 1969, modern social investing got its real start. The anti-apartheid movement in South Africa, large industrial actions against companies perceived as racist or anti-community, Ralph Nader's book *Unsafe at Any Speed* and the reaction by General Motors further fanned the embers of SRI. During this same period (1969–1971) the Interfaith Center on Corporate Responsibility (ICCR) was created and fought battles with corporations on their behaviour via proxy resolutions. ICCR is now active in developing broad-based corporate governance policies for companies through the publication of *Principles for Global Corporate Responsibility: bench-marks for measuring business performance.*[3] The genie was out of the bottle.

The most important by-product of a values-driven investment policy is that these funds performed better over a long period of time. By eliminating liability and risk, true insight into a company's potential became clear. More

[2] ibid
[3] *Principles for Global Corporate Responsibility: bench-marks for measuring business performance,* ICCR and ECCR and TCCR

recent studies such as *Built to Last*,[4] *Contented Cows Give Better Milk*[5] and the Kienbaum study[6] all quantified effects of a CSR programme on the value of a company.

1. *Built to Last* revealed that investments made in a values-driven company out-performed competitors that were not values-driven by 1,500%, over a 70-year period.
2. *Contented Cows Give Better Milk* showed profitability of 300% higher for 'contented cow companies' compared to their common cow counterpart over a 10-year period.
3. Kienbaum proved performance improvements of 200-350% for companies that showed high levels of co-operation, complementary communication, trust (lack of supervision) and high ethical standards.

The heir to the Baskin-Robbins fortune said: 'Prosperity based on pollution is not prosperity. It is short-term profit, long-term disaster.' With the success of screened fund, such as Domoni Index, ASN Trouw Index, Calvert, Pax and countless others, and the massive growth of SRI funds (nearly US$2,000 billion in the US alone), the financial community has woken up. Most major banks and investment houses have created or are creating products based upon some type of social and/or environmental criteria. This is combined with the latest European and Australian pension legislation, where SRI (Socially Responsible Investing) has been added to lawbooks. In the UK, requirements are made to be transparent about a pension fund SRI policy. This has achieved more than mandating social investing. As a result of this development, corporations will have to provide greater insight into social and environmental performance. This forces companies to create mechanisms to quantify their social and environmental risks, which creates a CSR momentum that builds each year and puts pressure on non-compliant companies to change.

HRM demands have created several near meltdowns of companies due to poor management. During the Vietnam War, Dow Chemical was a major

[4] Collins, James, and Porras, Jerry, *Built to Last: successful habits of visionary companies*, Century Business Books
[5] Catlette, Bill, and Hadden, Richard, *Contented Cows Give Better Milk*, Saltillo Press
[6] Wilms, Ralph, *Care Invest: socially responsive equity trust*, Kienbaum study result

producer of Napalm, Agent Orange and defoliants. If one looks at Dow now, they are regarded as a champion of reduction of material use, waste and pollution. Their European Vice President, Claude Fussler, in his book *Driving Eco Innovation*[7], calls for progressive action of business to achieve factor 100 performance (in terms of less use of materials, energy and waste production). What created this amazing turn around? A major factor was Dow's inability to attract the 'best and the brightest', due to its war machine image.

Shell experienced a similar problem. The negative press arising from Shell's handling of the human rights abuses of the Ogoni people in Nigeria and the call for the sinking of the Brent Spar oil platform created a crisis of image. This resulted in a loss of pride by employees and a decrease in the flow of CVs from the next generation of upper management. People didn't want to be associated with a company that was perceived to be acting out of power and arrogance, without any perceived sense of social responsibility. Employees want to be proud of their employer. These types of image crises will result in reduced employee loyalty, performance and recruitment.

Social auditing has grown to become an important tool for measuring a company's social liability, with awards being given for the best. Accounting firms are moving rapidly to create knowledge centres to provide this service to their customers. KPMG's purchase of The Body Shop's auditing department only emphasizes the case. Other consulting firms are developing effective methods to provide insight into how internally healthy an organization is. Standardization and verification of reporting is needed for social audits to become entrenched in triple bottom line thinking.

In order to manage the most valuable asset one has to be able to measure it. Without any effort, the advocates of social responsibility have received natural support. Investors find reduced risk and better returns over a long period of time from companies that follow triple bottom line principles. This protection of investment creates pressure on companies to live up to a certain standard. People are following their conscience by withholding

---

[7] Fussler, Claude, *Driving Eco Innovation: a breakthrough discipline for innovation and sustainability*, Pitman Publishing

labour or effort if a company rejects its social responsibility. The vulnerability of large companies has never been greater.

The greatest challenge is not that CSR and SRI will not happen, but that it will happen and corporations are not prepared for it. When they finally respond to the financial and staff pressures, they will find that there are not enough qualified people to carry out the process of CSR institutionalization, within the time frame needed. That is a frightening thought.

Albert Einstein best summed up the interconnectivity of the world:

'Each human being is part of a whole, which we call the Universe, a part that is limited in space and time. Each experiences himself, his thoughts and feelings in a kind of optical illusion, as if he were separated from the rest. This illusion is our prison and restricts our humanity to our personal desires. It condemns us to give our affection only to those closest to us. Our task must be to release ourselves from this prison by expanding the range of our sympathies, until they embrace all creatures and the whole of nature.'

The moving escalator – embedding and underpinning CSR in an organization (a practitioner's contribution to CSR policy-making)

Tony Hoskins, the Virtuous Circle

The European Enterprise Agenda Summit was an important stepping stone, helping organizations – from both private and not-for-profit sectors – to understand Corporate Social Responsibility (CSR).

The issue that this chapter addresses is how we can ensure that the dialogue becomes more than a talking point within a business and instead is embedded and underpinned in an organization – becoming an integral part of the business management process.

This chapter was written following the summit, and was presented, in an outline form, to the Department of Trade and Industry (DTI)/Economic and Social Research Council (ESRC) workshop on CSR, which had as its purpose the submission of inputs to the DTI for its development of the new Companies Act. Whilst this workshop had academic overtones, it's important to stress that this chapter has been written from the standpoint of the practitioner, observing the practices and processes of many leading companies when they are contemplating introducing or extending CSR into their businesses.

FROM REACTIVE TO PRO-ACTIVE

One of the benefits of the current debate about CSR is that there are some businesses that have been leading the way, and whose outputs are often held up as examples for others to follow.

Companies such as Diageo and Shell have made dramatic strides in terms of establishing their business values, understanding their stakeholders' views, developing programmes that address these needs, measuring their impact and communicating them in a manner that builds the quality and reputation of their brands.

However, many businesses – both large and small – are at the very early stages, often responding to stakeholder pressure in a reactive manner. Throughout this chapter, when reference is made to businesses, this encompasses both 'for profit' companies and 'not-for-profit' organizations such as government, education bodies such as universities as well as the voluntary sector. In my opinion, there is a risk that CSR is assumed to involve only the 'for profit' sector, but I see as much need for CSR in the 'not-for-profit' world!

When we look at the driving forces for CSR implementation in a company, many of them tend to be reactive in nature. The following chart demonstrates that many CSR driving forces could be perceived to be the result of either legislative or consumer pressure, instead of a pro-active force within the company.

SOME OF THE FORCES DRIVING CSR

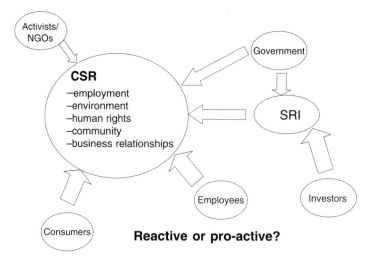

However, for CSR to become an embedded part of business process, it needs to move from being perceived as a reactive measure to become a pro-active programme.

To achieve this mind-shift, businesses need first to understand two key factors:

- They need to understand their values portfolio relating to their impact on the social economy – this should be the starting point for businesses to address their CSR positioning, but many businesses seem to start out on CSR without adequately reviewing their business values and their ethics.
- They need to understand on what areas their business activity could impact – for many businesses, the list of CSR issues in the large bubble on the left hand side of the chart includes areas that they do not yet recognize as being within their CSR programme.

The question is, how will businesses move from the reactive to the pro-active?

Currently, CSR seems to be the domain for large corporates, especially multinationals, often because non-governmental organizations (NGOs) and governments focus their attention on these bodies. However, for CSR to move forward, the domain needs to extend to large national companies, plus small and medium-sized enterprises (SMEs).

To do so, CSR needs to be brought to maturity as an integral business process – part of mainstream business thinking, rather than being perceived as a fad or the latest management buzzword.

The challenges in achieving this movement from the reactive to the pro-active lie in two areas. CSR needs to be put in the context of the business sector in which the business operates – there is no 'one size fits all' template for CSR! The CSR focus for a retail sector will be significantly different from that of a heavy manufacturing sector. But, I've observed that, even within the same sector, different businesses will have attained differing levels of CSR programmes. For many of them, their programmes will remain single focus – often related to the environment, because this is where the legislative pressures occurred first. At the same time, a few businesses will have already moved to multi-focus CSR programmes, covering the whole range of social, environmental and economic impacts upon society. Prime examples of such businesses tend to be the leading edge businesses, such as Diageo, Shell and now Marks and Spencer's. These companies may have had some 'earth shattering' event that led them further and faster along the CSR trail, but they are now prime examples because they have both multi-focus programmes and measurement activity in place. As a result they are communicating their achievements as a means of both addressing the stakeholders' needs and building their corporate brand reputation.

To be part of mainstream business thinking, CSR needs to be integrated into business planning and measurement. For this to occur to any extent beyond a reaction to the latest legislation there needs to be a senior champion within the business. Ideally this would be the chief executive, but, if not, senior board level commitment is essential.

But for the CEO to treat CSR as part of his or her mainstream business thinking, the champion needs to be able to achieve two steps – to demonstrate the business case for CSR and maintain the CEO's attention on CSR.

DEMONSTRATING THE BUSINESS CASE

This is a big challenge for practitioners of CSR. This is because most CSR programmes involve business intangibles – examples include risk management, health and safety at work, employee morale and brand reputation. CSR does not lend itself to the traditional business case of which accountants and management consultants are so fond.

However, the CSR business case can be developed by focusing on the required outputs, measuring their changes and establishing causal relationships. An example of this is research undertaken into cause related marketing by Research International, on behalf of Business in the Community. This shows that the brand reputation of companies undertaking these programmes can be enhanced tangibly whilst these programmes are under way. In itself, the enhanced brand reputation could be the business case for such programmes. However, for CEOs seeking greater tangibility, the need is to establish the causal relationship between enhanced brand reputation and market share – and that's the bigger challenge.

However, in another area, the business case may be established through more traditional means. There is significant evidence that multinationals are beginning to use CSR as a pre-qualifying requirement for its Request for Quotation documents, and this is being replicated by government approaches. This delivers the 'negative sell' for the CSR business case – 'If we don't do CSR, we won't qualify for the business' – which can often result in the focus being sharpened considerably.

Demonstrating the business case is the first step in ensuring that CSR becomes an integrated part of business thinking.

MAINTAINING THE CEO's ATTENTION ON CSR

To achieve the integration of CSR, the CEO's attention to CSR needs to be maintained. In my experience, the best way of ensuring this occurs is if CSR is perceived to continue to deliver benefits as a series of moving targets.

Most important in this context is the need to avoid the 'badge approach' – sometimes known as 'been there, got the t-shirt', but in corporate terms better described as 'Achieved this, got the plaque in reception'!

Examples of the 'badge approach' include:

- ISO 9001 and 14001 (quality and environment friendly)
- Investors in People (employee friendly)
- The Two Ticks (disability friendly).

While these are extremely valuable 'badges' for businesses to achieve, they may suffer on two counts:

- often the process of measurement becomes the goal, rather than the activity itself
- once achieved, the badge seldom offers significant incentive for a business to improve its efforts in this activity.

Currently I see a risk that CSR will suffer this 'badge approach', with the potential there for businesses to describe themselves as 'CSR friendly' without treating CSR as a series of moving targets and developing continuous improvement programmes as a result. The areas in which I see CSR badges occurring include:

- The codes of practice – such as the ABI Guidelines on CSR. When reading these codes, I am struck by the words used – businesses need to 'ensure that …' or 'state the policy on …'. There are few measures involved, and the risk is that businesses will comply with the codes, rather than committing to them.
- The government legislation, of which one of the first was the Pensions Act. In this the Pension Fund Trustee is required to state the socially responsible investment policy for specific funds. Again, there is no commitment to having such a policy – indeed a totally acceptable answer could be 'We do not have a socially responsible investment policy'.
- Lastly, stock exchanges' socially responsible investment indices such as FTSE4Good and the Dow Jones Sustainability Index. Particularly with the FTSE4Good, the issue is the extent to which the criteria for entering the index are watertight, and the extent to which they encourage improvement once the business is a component of the index.

All of these suffer from being relatively static 'badges', while what is required is the means to help the CEO think of CSR as a 'moving escalator'.

THE MOVING ESCALATOR

Why use the term 'the moving escalator' in the context of CSR? Because it is important for a CEO to understand some key issues about moving into CSR:

- Once you're on the CSR escalator, if you try to jump off, you have to work harder with your stakeholders because they lose trust in your commitment to CSR.

- The further you go up the escalator, the more extensive your objectives become in their scope – and CSR becomes more integrated in your business planning.
- What's at the end of the escalator? – another escalator! CSR maturity means you need continuously to review your objectives and programmes.

If these are the key issues, how do you determine *where* you are on the escalator? There are three criteria:

- The extent to which the organization has moved from a single focus to a multi-focus CSR programme.
- The extent to which the organization measures the impact of its CSR

'THE MOVING ESCALATOR'

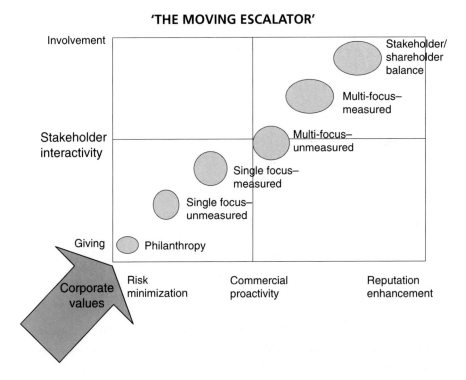

programme – not just *counting* the inputs, but *measuring the impact* on the stakeholders – especially their perception of the business's brand reputation as a result of the impact of the CSR programme.

● The extent to which CSR is integrated into businesses to achieve added value for the business.

In using 'the moving escalator' as a graphic illustration, there are two parameters or axes – the degree of stakeholder interactivity (moving from 'giving' to 'involving'), and the extent of commercial pro-activity (moving from 'risk minimization' to 'reputation enhancement').

The 'bubbles' ● on the escalator indicate how brand reputation value changes as a business moves along the CSR escalator. The large arrow in the lower left quadrant emphasizes that the first stage in determining the path a company wishes to take along the escalator is to determine the corporate values that underpin the business and its attitude towards CSR.

As a business moves along the escalator towards a more mature CSR approach, it moves from a basic philanthropic approach through first a single focus and then a multi-focus approach, developing measurements for each stage, until it achieves a balance between business value and stakeholder satisfaction – resulting in CSR integration into business planning.

It is important to recognize that for different sectors there will be different activities underlying the extent to which a business moves from single to multi-focus, and indeed, the smaller the business, the fewer the number of CSR focuses.

However, behind each step on the escalator, there are key indicators reflecting the extent to which the business has moved towards a sense of CSR maturity. These include the extent to which the CSR programme is:

● integrated into business plans
● expansive across all units of the business compared with a silo approach focused on individual units or departments of a business
● well communicated across all stakeholders
● market orientated, ie covering all environments in which the business

has an impact, compared with one which is orientated to a single site or a few sites

- multi-focused compared with a single-focused approach
- corporate led, ie embedded within the corporate culture, as distinct from one that is individual orientated, ie where one individual has a philanthropic approach that is yet to be adopted by the business as a whole
- measured (on a regular basis) in terms of the impact of the CSR programme upon stakeholders
- measured (on a regular basis) in terms of the impact upon shareholder Return on Investment (ROI).

These key indicators can be related to each phase of 'the moving escalator' as is shown in the chart below.

In conclusion, one of the key questions we have to ask ourselves is not only how do we ensure that CSR is given 'space' in a business but how can we ensure it is embedded and underpinned in businesses – beyond a token 'badge approach'?

CSR – 'THE MOVING ESCALATOR' AND THE KEY INDICATORS

	Stakeholder & shareholder balance	Multi-focus – measured	Single focus – measured	Philanthropy
Business plan integration	✓			
Expansive	✓	✓	✓	
Integrated communication	✓	✓	✓	✓
Market orientation	✓	✓	✓	
Multi-focused	✓	✓		
Corporate led	✓	✓		
Stakeholder impact measured	✓	✓		
Shareholder ROI measured	✓			

Achieving CSR maturity in businesses – particularly across a range from small to large – is not easy. To do so will need a variety of mechanisms – regulation is necessary, but *not* sufficient.

To achieve embedding we will need to ensure the CEOs see CSR as pro-active. To achieve underpinning we will need to ensure that there is measurement, bench-marking and recognition/reward. As part of this underpinning we need tools like 'the moving escalator' and its associated key indicators so that businesses will not only claim to be corporately socially responsible, but will also be able to identify where they stand in terms of corporate performance.

The role of socially responsible investment in CSR

Nick Wright, UBS Warburg

INTRODUCTION

However described, the issue of Corporate Social Responsibility (CSR) has risen rapidly up numerous agendas. Whether measured by conferences, articles or ethical funds under management, CSR has been the subject of phenomenal growth in comment, interest and practice. It has occasioned criticism from several quarters, for instance from both economist David Henderson and the journalist and writer George Monbiot. Whilst lack of agreement as to what CSR actually constitutes continues to be an issue, in the current economic and political environment questions are being asked as to whether CSR is a passing public relations fad or here to stay.

SOCIALLY RESPONSIBLE INVESTING/INVESTMENT (SRI)

According to the Social Investment Forum and the Conference Board, from 1997 to 1999 (the last date for available data) assets in all segments of social investing – screened portfolios, shareholder advocacy and community investing – grew 82% to US$2.16 trillion, representing about 13% of the US$16.3 trillion under professional management in the US. By way of comparison, the 82% growth rate of Socially Responsible Investing (SRI) is about twice the growth rate of all assets under management in the United States. Moreover, the trend is not confined to the US.

The market provides a mechanism for rewarding companies that behave in (whatever may be agreed as) a responsible fashion. The rapid expansion of the market for SRI suggests that either people/institutions wish to invest their money in responsible companies or they believe doing so will deliver equal or superior returns to the alternatives. If the latter is the case, a 'virtuous circle' will be created whereby the market delivers the incentive for companies to adopt socially responsible practices.

The evidence now as to whether or not SRI delivers superior returns is inconclusive. Among the arguments of those who believe it does, the following reasons have been advanced. CSR:

- is a sign of quality management
- contributes to reputation enhancement and brand promotion
- is the by-product of financial success
- reduces legal risk and litigation costs
- generates operating efficiency
- signals management's confidence in the future prospects of the firm.

The growth data cited above does not cover a sufficient time frame to allow the drawing of firm conclusions. However, there can be little doubt of the momentum behind SRI or that this niche market will become mainstream if the virtuous circle mentioned above is created, whatever the causal links proposed.

CONCLUSIONS

SRI has gathered pace as new laws and regulations have come into force and sentiments have changed. The advent of new indices will also no doubt add impetus to the growth of SRI and associated financial products. Nevertheless it seems unlikely, given current portfolio theory, that SRI confers any sustainable performance advantage in the long run. It does not appear to be the case, however, that SRI necessarily entails making financial sacrifices. This may be crucial. If it is indeed the case that 'doing good makes money' or at least does not cost money, who will not wish to adopt CSR practices?

CSR must have as its *raison d'être* the increase of value to the conventional bottom-line. If it does so or equals, through SRI, the performance of those funds outside its universe then surely it is here to stay.

Marketing social responsibility

Elisabeth Laville, Utopies (laville@utopies.com)

Business is in the driving seat of the sustainability transition: it has become the most powerful force in our societies and its capacity to effect social change is now proven.

At the same time, there is a growing concern about its social, environmental and cultural impacts, and marketing is a major focus for those who are questioning brand hegemony and corporate power – hence the world-wide success of *No Logo* by Naomi Klein, the book that became a symbol of the movement against corporate globalization and gave rise to the sub movement of 'culture jamming'.

Indeed, there seems to be an inherent contradiction between marketing and social responsibility, since marketing is mostly perceived as focused on private greed (ie sales, profit and increased consumption), while sustainability implies a focus on the public good. This means thinking about people rather than profits and minimizing negative impacts, such as the unsustainable use of natural resources, waste generation and the increased gap between the rich and the poor etc.

Whenever a company seems to be marketing (and especially advertising) its social responsibility, most people (including the media and NGOs) will question its true purpose, assuming that in the end business is more interested in building a socially responsible image than in really switching to socially responsible practices.

Defining under which conditions it is possible to market social responsibility is therefore a key issue in the sustainability transition because marketing is such a vital component of what business is about – bringing innovative products onto the market, building brand loyalty and reputation, answering people's needs, improving the global quality of life, educating consumers and promoting consumption patterns.

And the good news is that the only way to market social responsibility is to walk the talk, ie to switch to socially responsible marketing so that people do not question the company's commitment or wonder whether it is serving the cause or using it.

SO WHAT SHOULD BE DONE?

The classic 'Ps' of marketing have been irredeemably compromised. Products have become the symbols of useless consumption of non-renewable resources and the exploitation of workers. Promotion contributes to over-consumption. Packaging equals useless waste. Price is unfair for the producer as well as for the consumer. Marketing needs to be redesigned around the 3 'Ps' of sustainability – People, Planet and Profit.

If marketing is about answering people's needs, then we have to take into account new needs expressed by customers. Some 44% of European consumers are ready to pay higher prices for socially responsible products and 58% agree that companies are not doing enough in that field – MORI, 2000.

Companies must enter the virtuous circle of socially responsible marketing, by which the brand does well by doing good, thus creating a mutually rewarding relationship with its stakeholders.

This means that marketing must be redesigned to become more values-led than cause-related, ie use all aspects of marketing and communication to effect social, environmental and educational change (cf Eroski, The Body Shop, Migros, Working Assets, The Co-operative Bank, Benetton). An honest and long-term relationship with customers must be built and education, public awareness and training must be promoted, especially to the young. Additionally, information that is made avaliable to aid decision-making must be broadened and made more accessible. Success in marketing must be redefined not just in terms of products or profit but also in terms of service, reputation, relationships etc. All the social, environmental and cultural impacts of marketing choices should be assessed.

CONCLUSION

We must ensure the accountability of business by making corporate charters compulsory and asking companies to give details about how they intend to contribute to the public good. For corporations are supposed to be under people's ultimate authority, not the other way around.

When any corporation continually harms, abuses or violates the public trust, citizens should have the right to initiate a process that could revoke the company's charter, cause it to disband, sell off its enterprises to other companies and effectively put it out of business.

We must make prices reflect costs: the market doesn't provide consumers with proper information today. In order for a sustainable society to exist, every purchase should reflect or at least approximate its actual cost, not only the direct cost of production but also the cost to the air, water and soil; the cost to future generations; the cost to workers' health; and the cost in terms of waste, pollution and toxicity.

Thus we need to shift to a tax system that stops taxing what we want to encourage – jobs, creativity, payrolls and real income – and ignoring the things we want to discourage – environmental degradation, pollution and depletion. The entire tax system could be incrementally replaced by green fees – taxes that are added on to products, energy, services and raw materials, so that prices more closely approximate true costs.

Finally, we must support and initiate efforts to educate people about sustainable consumption and what it really means.

Tackling Exclusion Through Enterprise-Led Renewal

Ed Mayo, the New Economics Foundation

Over the last ten years, the New Economics Foundation and other agencies across Europe have helped to coin the term 'financial exclusion' and build an understanding of the debilitating impact it has for enterprises if they are cut off from credit and for people if they can't save, borrow and pay bills. Over a more recent period, banks have started to respond.

The first response from the banks was that this was an inevitable by-product of an efficient and competitive industry. Banking was all about selection, so you could not and should not try to reduce exclusion. Later, as evidence mounted, the second response was that 'yes', exclusion was a social concern, but that banks were not charities, so it was not down to them – except insofar as they were getting more competitive so would deliver to more people.

Politicians, under pressure from constituents, did not buy this and the position of banks shifted again. 'Yes', it was a charitable issue. Banks are highly competitive and socially responsible corporations and want to play their part voluntarily in alleviating the problem.

All this talk, including about how competitive the sector is, misses the point – which is that these are under-served markets, and that banks may be missing a profitable trick. Rather than agonize or whinge, some are now getting on with what they are best at, learning about this market and how to operate profitably in low-income areas.

The Inner City 100 is an attempt to help entrepreneurs in those areas make the case. The index will identify the fastest growing enterprises located in inner city areas. The Inner City 100 is led by the New Economics Foundation and supported by the Royal Bank of Scotland and NatWest. The unique mix of partners also includes HM Treasury, the Small Business Service, the Bank of England, the London Business School and the East Midlands Development Agency.

Tom Bloxham's Urban Splash has created a successful business in Manchester and Liverpool out of rehabilitating old buildings and providing mixed uses that combine leisure, workspace and living space. They have grown dramatically from a standing start in 1993 to being a major development force in two conurbations. Their recent schemes, such as the £50 million Brittania basin scheme in Castlefield, Manchester, and three developments in Liverpool together worth £28 million on the Collegiate site, the tea factory and the match factory illustrate the scale of their ambition.

They have shown that the inner city is an area of opportunity and can be a sound investment. The Inner City 100 will help other businesses to take a fresh look at the inner city. All too often written off as problem areas to be solved by someone else, inner city residents and entrepreneurs are proving the opposite.

Inner city areas are likely to be growth markets of the future. E-commerce, out-sourcing and modern, just-in-time competition all enhance the value of inner city locations. In a tight labour market, a number of alert employers are seeing the benefits of recruiting staff from inner city areas.

Equally, by rebuilding healthy local economies, inner city entrepreneurs are creating new opportunities and employment right now where it is most needed. Some £3 billion of public funding goes on regeneration each year, with undoubted benefits. But public money by itself has not been effective at restoring markets and renewing local economies. The emerging new paradigm of neighbourhood renewal starts instead from a recognition of the talent and potential of local people.

'Putting the spotlight on success is the best way of encouraging others' as Charles Handy, management guru and best-selling author, said after the launch of the Inner City 100.

Interestingly, success is not limited to private enterprise. The first company nominated for the index, by venture capitalist Sir Ronald Cohen, was the Furniture Resource Centre (FRC).

FRC is one of the fastest growing social enterprises in the UK. It has increased its turnover by 550% over the four year period 1996–2000 measured by the index. At the same time, its use of grant money has fallen from 80% of turnover to 9%. FRC specializes in providing low cost quality furniture to social landlords and other housing providers. Much of its product line is from recycled goods collected by Bulky Bob's, a wholly owned subsidiary with long-term contracts for house clearing and large item collection with Liverpool City Council and other social landlords.

FRC has expanded geographically and into new sectors. A key expansion was the setting up of CREATE in Speke, a specialist recycler of fridges and washing machines. FRC has also started to move beyond its Merseyside heartland into other parts of the UK. FRC shows all the hallmarks of an Inner City 100 nominee: growth, innovation and enterprise.

The Inner City 100 is constructed on the basis of nominations of enterprises like FRC operating in targeted areas. The starting cities are Bradford, Birmingham, Bristol, Coventry, Glasgow, Leeds, Leicester, Liverpool, London (Hackney, Newham, Haringey, Islington, Southwark and Tower Hamlets), Manchester, Newcastle, Nottingham, Salford, Sheffield and Sunderland.

These companies will be nominated for the index or can nominate themselves. The hope is that businesses, business associations, local authorities, voluntary organizations, MPs, Regional Development Agencies and Small Business Service outlets will nominate businesses in their areas.

To qualify the company must:

- be situated inside eligible postcodes in the 15 cities
- be independent (no other company holds a major share except venture capital)
- have a turnover of more than £25,000 in 1996 and £300,000 in 2000
- have created jobs between these years and employed at least five people in 2000

● act in a socially and environmentally responsible manner.

The benefit of the index will be felt by the inner city entrepreneurs running the successful enterprises, bringing them recognition, profile, active support and, in turn, increased sales.

Of course, not all inner city areas can boast an array of growth enterprises. There are significant differences between neighbourhoods such as south Hackney, which has a high number of businesses, and estates such as Braunstone in Leicester, which has few enterprises, many struggling to hang on. Different approaches will be needed on outer estates that were always dependent on jobs in nearby factories and which became enterprise deserts after the large-scale closures of the early 1980s.

Banks are an important component of success or failure. Seventy-two per cent of small firms use cash flow to fund their operations, so operate with short horizons and the risk of constant fluctuation. The challenge is to nurture a culture of enterprise with patient capital and to support young, private companies without driving them to become uprooted from their communities.

The Inner City 100 comes at a time of growing policy support for disadvantaged areas. The National Centre for Neighbourhood Renewal is up and running. The Bank of England now publishes an annual report on Finance for Small Businesses in Deprived Communities. The UK Budget contained a series of tax benefits for urban regeneration. One Treasury proposal out on consultation, developed by the New Economics Foundation, is for a Community Investment Tax Credit. This would offer a tax credit for investment in inner city enterprises. A £50 million tax credit could lever in an estimated £1 billion of investment and create 100,000 jobs.

The Chancellor has also earmarked £20 million to match £20 million of private investment for a new Bridges Community Development Venture Fund, again for inner city investment. In the words of Sir Ronald Cohen, who chaired the Social Investment Taskforce, 'the potential now exists to achieve a transformation of investment flows to support entrepreneurial value creation in those communities which have been most deprived of capital and management expertise.'

All of this activity offers inner cities the best chance in a decade of escaping a cycle of deprivation. If it works, it will also offer the banks the very best of reasons for engaging pro-actively in the cause of enlightened self-interest.

Cities And Quality Of Life
Jean-Pierre Worms, Laboratory of the Future

Eighty per cent of the world's population is 'urbanized'. Thus, most of the problems the world will face tomorrow – in the form of cultural, social, economic and political fragmentation and corrosion of the social fabric – are concentrated in cities.

Most of the resources needed to deal with such problems are also to be found in cities: economic resources (large enterprise, business and financial institutions and services), human resources (educational, professional training and research facilities), social resources (networks of 'social capital') and political resources (sophisticated systems of government, public utilities and services).

Historically, 'European civilization' was born and developed in 'cities'. The European challenge, in this area, is to harness such rich but diversified capital into a new synthesis from which to build a desirable future.

There are rising inequalities of access to all the necessary tools of city integration: education and cultural ability, jobs and economic capacity, use of public goods and services, political participation and active citizenship. To which, one should add the negative results of cumulative social, spatial and ethnic segregation. City fragmentation results in the following vicious circle: negative images stigmatize people and areas, and induce quantitative and qualitative disinvestment both from the public and private sector where positive action should take place. Such a spiral of exclusion breeds closed communities, social distrust and violence, including fundamentalism.

ON THE OTHER HAND

There is an enormous amount of individual and collective social energy, initiative and innovation mobilized in survival strategies which can be channelled into strategies of integration in the community, both socially and economically. The question is how to do it?

Cultural diversity can be a factor of innovation and development when bridges are built between communities and intercultural strategies constructed.

However, such innovative and determined action requires very imaginative social engineering in order to build working partnerships linking civil society, public government and private interests.

Numerous examples of successful innovations exist that deal with specific aspects of city reunification. All of them are based simultaneously on empowerment of deprived citizens by improving access to private initiative and public goods/facilities; opening up structures and methods of government and business investment in the community – micro credit, barter systems and time banks, facilities for local initiatives in job creation and start-ups – and encouraging intercultural activities and media; participative democracy etc. Few, however, are integrated into a global urban reconstruction strategy; this remains a new frontier for the 2Ist century.

The Laboratory of the Future aims to build such multi-sided partnerships around concrete projects in local urban communities. These partnerships include representatives of residents (civil society), of economic private interests (local small companies) and institutions (local, national and international authorities). Such programmes are taking place in various countries around the world (eg Bangladesh, Brazil, Senegal) and we have been exploring similar approaches in France.

Sustainable development of an enterprise is linked to the sustainable development of its direct environment (the local community) and of society at large. Such mutual interests between enterprise and society need to be implemented in concrete projects linking enterprise, civil society and government.

Derived from our dealings with problems of city reconstruction, the following recommendations for implementing the strategy would be stressed:

- If urban development is to be sustainable and successful, there must be an organized common strategy for all concerned, ie innovators, government departments, local associations, economic and financial institutions. This implies building new bridges between them so that they may work together on common goals.

- Thus 'social capital', as defined by Robert Putman (the Harvard Professor of Sociology) – networks plus shared perceptions, norms and values that facilitate co-operation in common endeavours – must be recognized as constituting, together with financial capital and human capital, the main resource of urban development. However, it can only thrive if hinged on concrete projects where all involved parties can see clearly what they can gain, ie in very explicit win-win achievements. Construction of such projects is therefore the main objective of the strategy.

- Upgrading local skills is a necessary preliminary: the specific resources of the residents and local communities involved must be identified, recognized and enhanced in deliberate 'empowerment' policies before a balanced and meaningful partnership can be built.

- Business managers and members of their executive bodies must have personal, direct contacts with the situations and people they are getting involved with in such innovative partnerships. 'Seeing is believing' and 'on-site visit' programmes are necessary for government and business leaders to change their understanding of the situation and of their future partners.

- In dealing with problems of unequal access to public and private goods and services, 'affirmative action', aimed at empowering the players of a game in which all players obey the same rules, should be preferred to 'positive discrimination', in which different rules apply to different players, according to their different initial capacities, eg quotas and various forms of lower standards for the disadvantaged.

The Kaos Pilots

Kaj Voetmann and Lars Mortensen

CREATING COMPETENT CITIZENS IN DEMOCRACIES IN A GLOBAL WORLD

In a globalized world we become interdependent. We all have to understand what this entails in order to be competent citizens in this world. 'Think global and act local' is the easy way to tell the message. In order to do this we have to change many of our ideas. We need to change our understanding of effectiveness and leadership. Effectiveness has to move towards sustainable development and leadership will have to move towards dialogue in networks. Another big challenge is the emerging knowledge economy.

There will be a need for redefining democracy where these two ideas – effectiveness and leadership – will be the basis for the interactions between global, transnational, national and regional institutions and local decision-making. There will be an ongoing discussion about where decisions have to be made and how to do it. This discussion will have to find a new balance between centralized and local decision-making.

If we want competent citizens they have to be engaged in the discussions that affect their lives. In a democracy that means they have to know how the system works in order to make good decisions. And the institutions need to create the framework for good local decisions. This can be achieved by supplementing the representative democracy with a network of conversations where all citizens are invited to participate in the policy development. The key to this will be all the people who are role models for our future generations: the teachers, the leaders, the politicians and all the adults.

SUSTAINABLE DEVELOPMENT THROUGH PARTNERSHIPS

Competent citizens need to know how to create sustainable development. It is fundamental in a sustainable region or country in a global world, that the citizens understand: that we all live in mutual interdependence; that we have a common responsibility for the exhaustible resources; that partnerships pave the way for a sustainable society; and that there has to be a high degree of feedback in these partnerships. To cope with this challenge all citizens must be flexible and be able to handle multiplicity.

People, institutions, enterprises and communities need to develop *mutual interdependence* in order to live in a sustainable way.

Common responsibility for exhaustible resources is necessary to make sure that there is sustainable production, sustainable consumption and a sustainable society.

The natural way to organize the creation of a sustainable society is by partnerships. The dynamic development in the world makes it necessary for people, institutions, enterprises and communities to learn to develop together. This is only possible if these partnerships build on democratic ways of working, where people, institutions, enterprises and communities experience the fact that they have real influence in the decision-making process and have the right to do things without asking (empowerment).

These partnerships can only thrive if there is a high level of feedback between the parties. It is this feedback that makes it possible to learn and develop together. People need to be flexible in order to react to the feedback and they have to be able to cope with multiplicity because the feedback will come from many different sources.

Flexibility is necessary if the parties are to be able to learn and develop together with the other parties in the partnership. But the partnership will only function if each of the parties is able to:

- Work in many relationships across borders between generations, ethnic groups, industries, professions and in lots of other ways to create bridges between parts of society.
- Work with the existence of many different ideas about how to do things.
- Make the multiplicity of the partnerships become a strategic resource, where society is alive because it is carried out through the relations between the different parts of society.
- Make sure that nobody is isolated, whether it be individuals, groups, institutions, enterprises or communities, because this isolation could become the source of prejudice and conflict, which would undermine the sustainability.

An even stronger way to create a sustainable society is by creating *symbiotic partnerships*. In a symbiosis two or more organisms live closely together, even inside each other. From biology we know that it is the symbiosis that creates new kinds of life. In the development of society it is symbiotic partnerships between independent units that creates innovation in products, organizing, co-operation and management. That is why co-operation has a central role in the development of individuals, institutions, enterprises and communities. But it is when the co-operation becomes symbiotic that things really start to happen.

Symbiotic partnerships are the answer to co-operation between education and enterprises in the future. On the way to creating symbiotic partnerships, institutions and enterprises have to learn to:

- look at each other as potential partners of co-operation
- involve each other in finding solutions with mutual benefits
- create growth through partnerships.

DEMOCRATIC DIALOGUES

Democracies based on sustainable development will have to create structures and methods that promote symbiotic partnerships. Democratic parliaments and councils must provide the framework that nurtures these

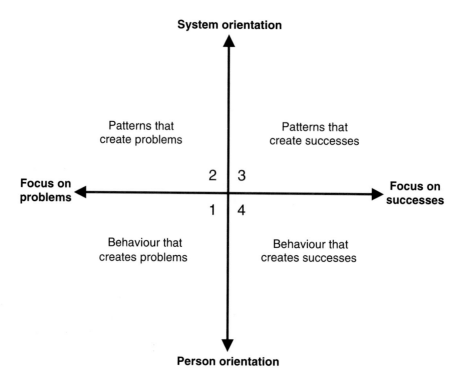

partnerships and they must be willing to listen to the decisions made in the local community.

Government and public institutions must be servants of the local communities and keep shaping themselves according to the wishes emerging from local democratic dialogues.

A very important discussion is how to create a flexible system that can handle multiplicity. This is connected to how we analyze what happens and what we want to create. Here is a framework for understanding this challenge.

In sustainable development we work in an ecological system, where it is important to create the right kind of feedback mechanisms. The figure above shows four different approaches to development. In the lower left hand corner we focus on people who are acting incompetently. The solution will tend to be based on inflexible rules that make several groups a problem and thereby keep them outside the democratic dialogues.

In the top left corner we look at the patterns and systems we have created that create the problems. In ecological systems this approach can be seen as negative feedback loops, which characterize declining systems. Here there is a tendency to organize things, which reduces the flexibility and thus reduces the ability to handle multiplicity.

By focusing on the top right corner we can start to talk about the patterns and systems that generate success, which is required to create competent people in a democratic society in a global world. This method will produce flexible systems based on self-organization and dialogue between many different groups and individuals. Finally, the bottom right hand corner looks at the behaviour that is necessary in order to maximize the effectiveness of the patterns described above.

This is where we need to focus if we really want to create competent citizens. We believe that 'Appreciative Inquiry' is one of the best approaches to create competent citizens. Appreciative Inquiry is a method and set of ideas that is based on action research and which can help people build the future they want together in a global world. In Appreciative Inquiry we deliberately choose to talk about things in a constructive, democratic dialogue between the parties who will be affected by the choices made for the common future.

'Open Space Technology' is another method that invites people to a democratic decision-making process, which makes it possible to find sustainable solutions to many of the topics that have to be handled in local communities. This has to be supplemented with a code of behaviour for people who engage in decision-making:

- There has to be an open invitation to the meeting for everyone who will be affected by the decision.
- Solutions and ideas have to be circulated to as many people as possible to get input at the meeting.
- Solutions must not be harmful to others.
- Solutions must make a better use of exhaustible or scarce resources.

- All actions must be taken in order to create a better future for humans and the environment now, and in the future.

EDUCATION

Education is the fundamental strategy that leads to a more dynamic, sustainable and equitable economy.

It is through education that we create the citizens of the future. We need to start by educating the educators in competence development based on the core competencies the citizens of the future need to master.

Some of the most important competencies everyone needs to master are those of:

- creating meaning for themselves, together with other people
- creating relationships with other people
- learning individually and together
- changing individually and together.

These have to be supplemented by professional competencies.

An Arts And Business Enterprise Strategy For Europe

Colin Tweedy, Arts & Business

Arts & Business is the world's foremost organization building links between the commercial and cultural sectors. Our mission is to help build communities by developing creative partnerships between business and the arts. Since 1976, Arts & Business has worked with thousands of businesses and arts organizations, helping them to build creative partnerships that deliver mutual benefits. While we initially focused on business sponsorship of the arts, we now advocate and encourage multi-faceted partnerships that are profitable and sustainable in the long term.

Working with a thousand volunteers from leading businesses, we manage professional development programmes that facilitate the sharing of skills and experiences between managers from business and the arts. We also facilitate this flow of expertise in the opposite direction, by helping artists to use their unique talents to inspire creativity and innovation within business.

Since Arts & Business was established in 1976, the total value of business investment in the arts in the UK has risen from £600,000 to over £150 million per annum, and over £1 billion of business investment has been generated for the arts. This has levered substantial benefits for both the cultural and commercial sectors and, crucially, has helped strengthen the wider community.

CURRENT STATUS OF THE CULTURAL DEBATE

The restriction on space makes it impossible to lay out the argument in the detail it deserves at this stage. We have chosen instead to focus on the main challenges that we believe face the business, public sector and arts worlds in measuring up to the current social and economic challenges.

Challenges:
- To place a dynamic cultural policy within government and business thinking.
- To equip the cultural sector with the business and civic skills needed to operate within a sustainable entrepreneurial context.
- To broaden the market's profit motive to include social and community profits, individual profits, creative profits and sustainable profits.
- To equip business with creative skill sets and learning systems that embrace risk, change and individual genius.

Needs:
- A safe and open environment for meeting, discussing and building relationships between the key players.
- Improved policy co-ordination of cultural issues amongst national administrations and multilateral bodies (including the European Commission and the Council of Europe).
- Detailed action research (econo-metric and social) which brings together the story of culture and its social, environmental and economic impacts on various societies.
- Detailed case studies and an advocacy plan for the cultural dimension of development.
- Funding for pilot projects, evaluation and refined case studies.

We believe that the cultural sector offers an example of the triple win in action – private gain as employees and investors, public value for audiences and communities, and social benefits for individuals and groups at risk. However, very few of the ways in which the arts are relevant to a wider entrepreneurial strategy in Europe have been recognized or explored.

Arts & Business sees the opportunity for new radical thinking about the role of the cultural sector falling into two distinct areas:

1. CULTURAL INITIATIVES CONTRIBUTING TO A DYNAMIC ENTREPRENEURIAL SOCIETY

This view works from the proposition that the arts and heritage are full economic players in their own right, as well as effective tools for the development of key entrepreneurial skill sets in the 21st century. Some of these 'initiatives' do or should include:

- **Profitability.** Culture as a contributor to local, national and European GDP. Its role as a motor of tourism. The impact of high culture on service industries such as the hotel and restaurant trade. The influence of popular culture on fashion, music and politics. The relevance of culture in urban and rural regeneration. The growth of the culture industries (design, graphics, audio-visual, music, service sector) and its roots in high arts training or provision.
- **Innovation.** The role of the arts in providing innovative responses within industry (Levi's, Apple, Unilever) or within localities and regions (Barcelona, south London, Rotterdam). Some of these innovations depend on arts techniques and attitudes being grafted within another culture (arts-based training), some on the stimulus of artists working within their own environment (in arts clusters such as the Jewellery Quarter, Birmingham). Artists are living case studies of what makes innovation possible, and how to create environments conducive to small-scale initiatives that support risk and encourage growth.
- **Civic actors and social entrepreneurship.** The arts act as powerful role models for civic and individual change, not only through their aesthetic and spiritual impact, but also through training, participation and joint problem-solving. Arts organizations and artists are social entrepreneurs who work with creativity as a basic tool. Creating economic opportunity also depends on retaining a sense of personal

responsibility, a can-do attitude and networks of support. The arts approach to success (competitive collaboration) may provide some links and suggestions for new ways of encouraging economic and social entrepreneurship.

2. CULTURAL SOLUTIONS TO SOCIAL AND ENVIRONMENTAL ISSUES

This view works from the proposition that the cultural sector responds to social challenges via value sets that put the individual firmly within a community or group context. The arts and heritage sectors are about both tradition and innovation, group solidarity and individual genius. For this reason they are increasingly important social players in communities across Europe.

- **Social cohesion.** Culture contributes to social cohesion by working on three levels of relationship. Culture *builds* individual skills and capacities; culture *bonds* communities together around common themes and preoccupations that stress the positive and creative rather than the negative and reductive; culture also *builds* bridges between groups and communities with different agendas, creating respect for difference and awareness of common human issues.
- **Diversity and commonality** (high culture and local culture). Culture stresses the need for the specific human response to an issue while working on the themes common to us all. Music, theatre, arts and literature are windows into other world-views. Cultures that are difficult to access because of their policies or gender approaches can be approached via their music and art. Collectively the response to beauty, to ugliness and to emotions is similar, reinforcing our common destinies. Arts provide an ever-expanding language of human consciousness, between cultures, between races, between individuals, between generations and between localities.
- **Sustainability.** The arts work small-scale, short-term and in fragile economic conditions. Yet they have long-term, universal and shared goals. The environmental and social sustainability of projects is mirrored by their cultural sustainability, which is often defined in a different way

to commercial sustainability. An artist who fails at a project will start another. An artist is happy to accept that an approach, a language or a theme has a limited shelf-life and will explore new ways to achieve the same goal. The arts therefore require different financing mechanisms, call on different skills sets and produce results over different time frames, all of which are relevant to the business entrepreneur, especially in the early stages.

CONCLUSIONS

1. To bring together the various initiatives in the cultural sector in this area under a single, annual meeting. This 'Davos for the arts' would serve as an opportunity to collate information and ideas, tackle projects and initiate collective, creative innovation. Arts & Business is willing to act as convenor of such a meeting.

2. To avoid ghettoizing of the arts and culture in the wider debates by identifying an 'arts ambassador' to work with the Progressio Foundation and The Work Foundation to explore the point of contact between the cultural sector and the overall areas of debate.

3. To draw up an 'arts matrix' of the relationship between the arts and heritage sectors and the various themes identified within the European Enterprise Summit, plus case studies and research, for circulation to all attendees and as a blue-print for further action research and projects. This 'arts matrix' (which, depending on resources, might be Europe-wide) to serve as the basis for a policy document on 'the role of the arts in the European enterprise strategy', to be discussed within the main multilateral bodies (European Commission and the Council of Europe) and endorsed by The Work Foundation and the Progressio Foundation.

Appendix 1

Further contributions

The idea for this book arose from an initial summit meeting of predominantly, but not exclusively, European progressive entrepreneurs, activists and thinkers. What follows are key conclusions and recommendations made by some of the others who attended the European Progressive Enterprise Network inaugural summit meeting in London 4–5 November 2001.

Biopolitics – a framework and vision for environmental progress

Dr Agni Vlavianos-Arvanitis, President and Founder, the Biopolitics International Organization

Since its inception in 1985, the Biopolitics International Organization (BIO) has been emphasizing that environmental protection and respect for the gift of life must evolve into a more expansive concept and become part and parcel of the dominant social paradigm. The ethics of this endeavour involve a number of different elements and the solution lies in a deeper understanding of our responsibilities as human beings on this planet. Current environmental policy is based on the idea of sustainability. Although this idea consists of many aspects and operates as a first line of defence against environmental degradation, its long-term viability is not guaranteed. The flaws can be justified by the absence of an internationally agreed strategy and of a unified vision. A new strategy, which goes beyond sustainable development, can broaden our horizons and can introduce the necessary criteria for a more just and safe global management.

For the reversal of negative trends to be effective, and to avoid further degradation and catastrophe, environmental legislation has to be adopted universally. Threats to the environment (bios) do not recognize national borders, political and religious differences. However, these threats can be resolved through multilateral co-operation and through bio-diplomacy.

Society needs to mobilize every one of its elements and strive for a better future. We are now consumed in an inverted pyramid structure, where nothing is in balance because the right priorities have not been set. The pyramid may become re-inverted once we acknowledge the value of basing the entire structure of society on biocentric principles. The International University for the Bio-Environment (IUBE) – an initiative that actions the BIO aspiration for global environmental literacy – is a catalyst that can infuse society with these necessary models. It provides a new educational challenge, fighting the trend towards over-specialization and seeking to open up all areas of study and training to an appreciation of life on our planet.

The current crisis of values is a great threat, not only to the environment but also to peace. This is why there is a pressing need to use the diachronic ideals of the past to motivate every member of society towards the conservation of the environment. The 'Olympic Spirit' can play a leading role in uniting the forces of culture and technology to instil the appreciation of the aesthetic value of life on our planet. An 'Olympiad of Values' and not merely of physical prowess must evolve. Prizes for each speciality, with the participation of every individual and profession in the race to save the environment, is one of the major BIO goals for the new millennium.

Environmental destruction is still cheap because the environment has not been priced. Threats to the environment can only be relieved through a fundamental change in the economy. The issue of 'quality of life' needs to assume top priority, along with culture and education. These elements need to become the framework for the new economics of the 21st century. Moreover, the concept of profit has to be redefined and encompass elements that constitute a 'genuine' profit for society – culture, internal wealth, preservation of natural resources, better health and the protection of biodiversity – as a measurable part of a nation's prosperity.

BIO has been promoting the introduction of a 'green salary' for the unemployed, with the commitment to work for the protection of the bio-environment. Projects could include tree planting, city clean-up, recycling, resource recovery and other constructive activities. This green salary can help improve morale among the unemployed, in addition to providing new opportunities for work and helping to lower unemployment levels. Moreover, businesses could be granted special tax deductions when providing opportunities for the unemployed to be involved in environmental projects.

In this crucial endeavour, it is essential to have global participation and the time is ripe for humanity dynamically to voice its concern over environmental deterioration. A world referendum, where every citizen on the planet would simultaneously cast a vote for the environment, would result in a global mobilization for the reversal of destructive trends and would guarantee a brighter future.

To encourage international co-operation the world needs to stop investing in war and start investing in environmental preservation. Without interfering with vested interests, the greatest challenge for the 21st century should become the development of new ways of channelling current defence protocols so as to adopt the principle of *defence for bios* as the primary national and international priority. Existing defence equipment can be amended and used for re-forestation, water resource clean-up, soil erosion recovery, protection of the ozone layer and the de-contamination of areas affected by nuclear radiation.

The central concept of bio-legislation, regarded as an integral part of biopolitics, is to link the protection of bios rights to the defence of the rights of future generations. Furthermore, bio-legislation acknowledges that in addition to 'human rights' there exists a series of 'human obligations' geared towards our common responsibility to preserve the environment and improve quality of life on a global level. It is therefore essential for international legislation to make explicit reference to the protection of bios on our planet and for current environmental acts to be expanded upon and re-evaluated.

Environmental disasters point to the urgent need to establish an active international court for the environment, as already promoted by the International Court of the Environment Foundation and by members of the

Permanent Court of Arbitration and endorsed world-wide. It is essential to have a globally acknowledged council as a means for solving environmental disputes and ensuring global environmental responsibility.

Ethics in practice – developments and approaches in Germany

Annette Kleinfeld, Member of the European Business Ethics Network and Partner in Bickmann & Collegen Consultancy, Hamburg

The debate about business ethics in Germany has significantly changed during recent years, from a more or less academic debate in universities and research centres to a discussion about effective ways of developing, implementing and monitoring ethical orientations within companies.

This development is being reflected by the development of the German European Business Ethics Network (EBEN), the DNWE (Deutsches Netzwerk Wirtschaftsethik e.V.). Since its establishment in 1993, it has become the largest of the national EBEN networks with more than 500 members, including a growing number of institutional members from all branches of industry.

In Germany, the increasing interest of companies in business ethics has different roots. These include:

- A growing tendency to focus attention on the criminal actions and unethical behaviour of both managers and employees, where this is revealed.
- The debate about bio ethics (which in Germany cannot be discussed without the specific historical background of Nazi Germany) and its implications for biotech companies.
- The change of markets and the decreasing role of politics against a background of the processes of globalization which has led to an increase in corporate responsibility, especially of the so-called global player.

- The impact and consequences of globalization inside companies as a result of growing market pressure, orientation to stock markets and shareholder value, intercultural conflicts, new challenges for employees and managers as a result of new working conditions, a lack of orientation in diversified, global structures and networks etc.
- Increasing external pressure by critical consumers, by the public and even by shareholders in cases of unethical performance (Shell: Brent Spar. Bayer: Lipobay etc).
- A new generation of entrepreneurs in small and medium sized owner-driven companies, ie the relieving process of a generation of entrepreneurs who personally represented ethical and social values in their corporate conduct, thus founding the tradition of the social market economy in post-war Germany.
- Attempts by politicians and the major economic associations to renew this tradition, ie the concept of the social market economy in connection with today's concepts of 'good corporate citizenship', 'sustainable business conduct' or 'best practice in entrepreneurship'.

The initiatives of German companies in order to cope with these issues and ethical challenges in practice can be summarized under the following topics:

1. Integrity and risk management
2. Management of values
3. Cultural change/cultural integration programmes (eg in M&A processes).

Regarding the first two issues, the main approaches are aimed at developing guidelines/codes of conduct containing ethical principles and values in order to clarify the form and degree of ethical behaviour the company expects from all of its employees.

The next step is to ensure that these orientations are complied with and lived up to. A growing number of companies are implementing special management systems or programmes that help to implement and control the realization of their codes of ethics and corporate values.

The German EBEN network (DNWE), for instance, established its own 'Centre for Business Ethics' (ZfW) which has recently developed a standard of 'ethics management'. Companies following these standards can get audited and certified by the ZfW to encourage a continuous improvement process. Accounting companies like KPMG and PWC, which have been involved in developing this standard, are currently starting to promote it in their offers of compliance programmes and integrity services.

One disadvantage of most of the numerous ethical and social standards that have been developed in European countries during the last years, however, is that they have a merely national focus and perspective. Besides, most of them are not as flexible as they need to be in order to adjust both to the specific needs of different branches as well as to the specific corporate cultures of companies.

This means that appropriate standards or management systems in the field of business ethics have to be open to approaches that develop and shape cultures.

These would include:

- cultural analysis and values assessment
- development and implementation of vision, mission and code of conduct (including guidelines for branch specific issues and a stakeholder balanced management)
- deducing policies and strategies, goals and measures from these orientations
- continuous evaluation of deployment efforts and progresses (corporate controlling both by internal self-assessment and external audits/cultural analysis)
- establishing processes that ensure continuous cultural improvement (HR management, leadership development, symbolic management, event driven management etc).

EBEN is therefore developing a European model of managing ethical orientations in and of companies on the basis of the practical experiences of our members in almost all European countries – a model that should also be able to take into account both national and corporate cultural differences.

Corporate social innovation

Josep M Lozano, ESADE (Barcelona)

Corporate social innovation concerns responsibility framed in terms of inter-dependence. Nowadays, corporate responsibility is not merely a question of the consequences arising from corporate actions but refers to the way in which companies form part of, and act within, their network of relationships.

Corporate Social Responsibility (CSR) is reflected in the values and criteria that orientate all company relationships. This approach views companies as both social and economic actors. This recognition of companies' social role is not something that is additional to their business but rather something that imbues every aspect of their activities and affects the way they are understood. Companies need to assume this approach. The social behaviour of companies cannot be divorced from their economic behaviour – these are simply different ways of looking at the same corporate reality. Their deeds are open to judgement in both economic and social terms because firms make a decisive contribution to the way in which society is shaped. I believe that this is the real reason and justification for the triple bottom line and new forms of social auditing and accountability.

Accordingly, I believe we should go beyond social responsibility and start talking in terms of social innovation. This is not to say that the traditional concerns of social responsibility are no longer valid. Rather, it is that in a networked society, the ethics of co-responsibility demand greater and sounder social innovation. We need to commit ourselves in new ways and tackle new forms of organizational learning, new forms of social interaction, new capabilities for creating and sharing goals and values. It is a question not simply of discussing the consequences of our deeds but of deciding what we want to do and help to build – companies need to think in these terms because the kind of innovation required now no longer refers only to products, services and processes. We also have to learn how to foster institutional innovation with regard to values and attitudes. In the emerging new society, companies must learn how to construct their own legitimacy (something that can no longer be taken for granted) and decide how they want to be seen by others. Put another way, firms should be seen as laboratories for social innovation.

What does this mean in practice? I think there are five steps that should be taken:

- Create a different and more inclusive vision of globalization, not against corporations (or in spite of them) but with them.
- Avoid approaching social innovation only from the viewpoint of large multinationals and ensure the inclusion of SMEs.
- Learn how to foster dialogue among companies, public administration and not-for-profit organizations.
- Foster corporate communication and a mind-set targeted at society, ensuring the message also takes account of societal points of view rather than exclusively market-orientated ones.
- The opportunity must be grasped to increase companies' social legitimacy and commitment to their own people.

To achieve these ends we need to create the means. This involves creating business networks that cover social innovation processes. As a first step we must identify social innovation as a key element in corporate strategy rather than treating it as an operational or communications issue. We must develop companies' ability to grasp society (instead of just the market) as a way of drawing up commitments that are consistent with corporate missions and competencies. Finally, we must foster greater partnership and shared learning with universities, in developing a greater commitment to social innovation and organizational values, and incorporate these issues into corporate training plans.

This must form part of business strategy and management. We are discovering new forms of partnership and collaboration between organizations and institutions that hitherto regarded one another solely as rivals, competitors or obstacles to be overcome. This has important implications for the development of human resources and communication policies based on dialogue rather than on a single, one-track view.

The public affairs function as change agent

Tom Spencer, the European Centre for Public Affairs

The public affairs function exists on the boundaries between business, government and civil society. When operating properly, the public affairs function represents corporations to the world and, arguably more importantly, carries messages from the world into the corporations. It is key to the conduct of successful public affairs at this level that practitioners can analyze and anticipate change in the environment in which their companies operate. In successful companies, senior public affairs people have direct access to CEOs. Public affairs is also practised by civil society and the not-for-profit sector and, in a different way, by governments. The European Centre for Public Affairs (ECPA) programmes have established themselves as a safe space in which a serious analysis of decision-making can be entered into by all parties.

Good public affairs is intimately linked with the creation of corporate strategy and is a great deal wider than the act of lobbying. It has been rightly said that 'one lobbyist is an offence against the public good: but a hundred lobbyists are a guarantee of good governance'. Public affairs practitioners, whether corporate or from civil society, help to shape the democracies in which they operate. This is particularly the case in supra-national constructs, such as the European Union and the institutions of our emerging global governance. It would be a major contribution to enterprising Europe if the intelligence, energies and resources of the public affairs function could persuade senior management to be pro-active in strengthening the

European, and indeed the global, polis at this time of substantial institutional change and paradigm shift.

There is an urgent need to spread the best standards of public affairs practice. This is particularly important in the area of Corporate Social Responsibility (CSR), which is currently patchily pursued in the different national contexts of the European Union. It would be a huge advance if its current Anglo-Saxon popularity could be adapted and transposed for wider use in mainland Europe.

The public affairs function needs to overcome a continuing perception of being solely concerned with lobbying on behalf of the narrow interests of corporations. Corporations need to take a more responsible and holistic approach to their relations with, and duties to, society at all levels.

The current fluidity of European and global structures offers a major opportunity. A parallel might be drawn with the work of Counterpart in sponsoring 'analogue forestry'. Analogue forests, created in abused marginal forest land across the developing world, are not the same as natural, first growth forests. However, they mimic such forests on the basis of understanding the dynamics of natural forest growth. By extension, the institutions that we create at European or global level are not natural political structures in the sense we have become used to with nation states. There are, however, good and bad ways of creating supra-national institutions. As business comes to recognize that the fundamentalist rhetoric of 20 years of Davos is inadequate, it should take up its responsibilities to help shape transparent and democratic institutional frameworks. Corporations need to be encouraged not to replace governments, with all the attendant political risks, but to supplement governance.

SOME IDEAS AND SOLUTIONS

There are numerous examples of successful collaboration between business and civil society organizations contributing to good governance. The work of Unilever and WWF is an obvious case. The ECPA is currently seeking funding for a research project bench-marking the conduct of public affairs in six transnational corporations and six globally organized NGOs. Part of this research is designed to establish the boundary conditions of success in such creative collaboration.

There is an urgent need to package the various progressive initiatives currently being developed across Europe into a coherent and replicable strategy for every corporation. Current corporate involvement is patchy, nationally differentiated and sectorally diverse. Many companies find themselves in the potentially unstable situation of being good, or very good, at part of the CSR agenda, but correspondingly vulnerable to attack in areas that have not attracted their attention.

A strong public affairs input to the enterprise strategy would fit elegantly into the discussion initiated by the European Commission's White Paper on Governance in the European Union. In particular, there is an urgent need for the reform of EcoSoc and the updating of the Social Partners model in the European Union. There is a similar urgent need for creative business input into issues of global governance at a critical moment in the debate on globalization. Debate about the future of Europe can no longer be seen in isolation from global developments. The role of business think-tanks and organizations, such as the European Roundtable and the European American Industrial Council, need to be given greater focus if the enterprise strategy is to be a success.

There is an urgent need to increase the quality and quantity of public affairs education in management education generally. This should certainly involve the European Foundation for Management Development. Also, active practitioner participation in the creation of case studies for teaching purposes needs to be encouraged.

Finally, the debate about CSR needs to be more securely anchored in the debates about institutional change at European and global level.

The Centre for Tomorrow's Company

Mark Goyder, Director

The Centre for Tomorrow's Company (CTC) is a business-led think-tank and catalyst. It was founded in the UK, following the success of the RSA Inquiry into Tomorrow's Company, which developed the concept of an inclusive approach to business leadership. CTC now has an international influence and perspective.

Our vision and purpose is to create a business future that makes sense to staff, shareholders and society.

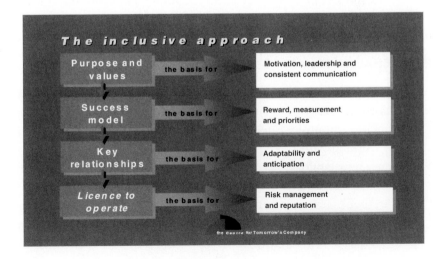

Our focus is upon leadership and governance. Our work is intended to influence five audiences:

- Business leaders
- Investors
- Business educators
- Stakeholder groups
- Public policy-makers.

Our strategic objectives are:

- To undertake and publish agenda-setting research, drawing upon the experience of business.
- To promote the adoption of new ideas, frameworks and agendas to further the vision.
- To recruit and mobilize members, partners and donors from among our chosen audiences to participate in our research and champion our values.
- To act as an inspiring focal point for business and our other audiences by facilitating debate, generating, linking and exchanging ideas, and encouraging learning.
- To identify and explore with business the future sources of durable and sustainable success.

NEEDS, CHALLENGES AND OPPORTUNITIES CURRENTLY FACED

- 21st century investment: an agenda for change. There is now widespread acceptance by business of the need for an inclusive approach. The investment community is felt by many to be an obstacle to its adoption. CTC is working with CEOs, fund managers and investment experts to develop a new language, accountability and time horizon to reflect the full range of consumers' needs and values.
- Measurement and reporting: the case for inclusive measurement frameworks has been made. The need now is to develop practical solutions that simultaneously reflect the needs of shareholders and other

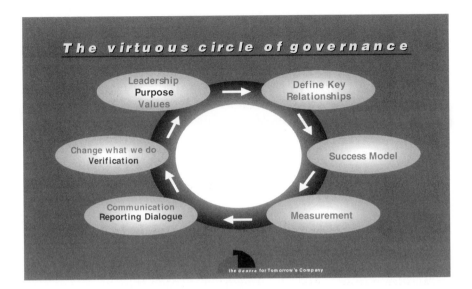

The virtuous circle of governance

stakeholders. (This cannot be achieved simply by using the triple bottom line, which reflects a company's external impacts rather than its business drivers.)

- Inclusive leadership: interpreting the changing business environment and making sense of the new economy; developing practical models of inclusive leadership which combine the creation of value for shareholders and society. Embodying an inclusive view in company governance, measurement and reporting, and modifying company law to reflect this. (See diagram above, 'The virtuous circle of governance'.)
- Alternative patterns of ownership: exploring the benefits of employee ownership and of other governance models, which heighten stakeholder commitment without jeopardizing necessary adaptiveness.
- International approaches to governance: stimulating and charting the convergence between Anglo-American and European models of governance. We need to redefine governance, which is about leadership and accountability, not simply the technicalities of board operations and controls.
- Reaching the mainstream: securing the adoption of inclusive business

leadership by the bulk of mainstream companies beyond the charmed circle of 'usual suspects'.

SUCCESSFUL SOLUTIONS AND STRATEGIES FOR PROGRESS (ALL SUMMARIZED IN RELEVANT PUBLICATIONS)

- An inclusive approach to sustainable and durable business success (see figure on p. 199) detailed in 1995 findings of RSA Tomorrow's Company Inquiry).
- An inclusive approach: the research evidence (published 1998; to be updated).
- An inclusive approach to company reporting to meet the needs of society and shareholders (see 'Sooner, Sharper Simpler' 1998 and 'Prototype plc' 1998).
- An inclusive approach to leadership ('Leadership in Tomorrow's Company' 1999 and 'Leading and Managing in the New Economy' 2001).
- An inclusive approach to directors' duties – (see 'The Corporate Reporting Jigsaw' 2000): the inclusive framework for reporting CTC's proposals in this area have been adopted in the UK proposals for the reform of company law.
- An inclusive approach to investment – (see Twenty First Century Investment: an agenda for change, published June 2001).

SYNERGIES AND CONNECTIONS WITH OTHER ISSUES OF THE ENTERPRISE STRATEGY

- 'What does Europe stand for?' and 'What is the constructive role for enterprise within European society?' are both questions that are closely aligned with CTC.
- Triple win for investors, enterprises and the public interest – maps exactly on to our vision and purpose.
- Balance between long-term and short-term, thought and practice is reflected in our membership and working method.

- Our quest is to develop a widely acceptable concept of the company, which reconciles the Anglo-American focus on shareholder accountability with the traditional European focus on society and employee accountability – at its heart is the inclusive concept that leaves each company free to define its own purpose and values but places values-based leadership and relationships at the heart of success.

Socially responsible enterprise restructuring and the new enterprise agenda for Europe

George Starcher, Founder, the European Baha'I Business Forum (EBBF)

A progressive entreprise strategy for Europe must deal with the way companies approach restructuring. Massive lay-offs and plant closures which are not accompanied by reponsible site rehabilitation simply have no place in such a strategy. A current joint project being carried out by the International Labour Office (ILO) and the European Baha'I Business Forum illustrates how restructuring can be carried out more responsibly and with fewer social problems and costs.

INTRODUCTION

Profits down or well below shareholder expectations? Competition eating into market share? Customers complaining about product quality or safety? Looking for synergy to justify a poor acquisition or merger? Maybe it's time to restructure, consolidate, tighten up …

Rarely are companies' business principles and codes of conduct tested as severely as when they 'restructure'. Nor do they know that most efforts involving lay-offs have such a serious impact on the health and lives of those affected: those laid off, their families, the remaining employees and the communities involved. And rarely do companies calculate or consider the substantial 'hidden costs' of downsizing such as the effects on morale, motivation, loyalty, turnover, absenteeism and quality – to name a few.

Few companies escape the need to restructure to cope with their turbulent environments and remain competitive and viable. Thus restructuring involves a number of major issues not only for managers of companies but also for various stakeholders: employees, customers, governments, communities, suppliers, shareholders and even environment.

What are these issues? How can companies restructure responsibly and balance the interests of the various stakeholders? What examples are there of 'best practices' followed by responsible companies? What are the social costs and the impact of massive lay-offs on employees and communities? Do the traditional across-the-board reductions really achieve their objectives? What is the role of government in defining the regulatory environment affecting restructuring? The ILO and EBBF launched a joint project to identify best practices and to develop and define socially responsible approaches and practices for restructuring.

CONCEPT DEVELOPMENT

Following an initial phase of desk research a report was published which developed the following basic concepts:

- The ways and means of restructuring must seek to minimize the social costs of restructuring such as dislocations, loss of jobs, deterioration of the quality of jobs, and a loss of social cohesion at work and in the community.
- Companies must remain competitive and profitable. Unprofitable companies cannot be socially responsible for very long.
- There is a hierarchy of ways of restructuring. The report advocates that higher, more strategic, levels of restructuring should be studied before decisions are made to downsize or reduce personnel costs.
- If staff reductions are really necessary, there are measures to achieve results without redundancies and lay-offs and, ultimately, ways to facilitate re-employment and reassure remaining employees.
- Governments, in consultation with employers' associations and workers' organizations, have an important role in defining the legal and regulatory environment within which managers decide whether and how to restructure.

FOLLOW UP

The working paper has led to the following steps being taken by the ILO and EBBF to promote responsible restructuring.

1. The findings were presented in a meeting of practitioners including managers, academics and consultants organized jointly at the ILO offices in Geneva.

2. The ILO is overseeing a computerized series of 12 modules, representing over 1,200 pages, of material for trainers, consultants and companies. It includes manuals, case studies, some videos and conceptual papers on such relevant issues as workers' buyouts, social aspects of mergers and acquisitions, workforce adjustment, worker-management co-operation in restructuring, crisis management and privatization. The resource pack aims to build consensus and the capacities of the social partners, managers and workers to pursue restructuring in a socially responsible way.

3. The ILO organized and led two-day seminars in over a dozen cities in Russia and the Ukraine. The ILO also conducted several two-week seminars in Russian at the Turin training centre, and translated and published a book in Russian.

4. The ILO has organized one- and two-week training seminars in their Turin training centre in English and Chinese for managers.

5. The EBBF has written and published a condensed version of the report in English and French. Some of its members have given presentations on the findings at conferences on CSR and at business schools.

6. The ILO is translating the condensed version into Chinese and is planning to introduce the concepts in Asia (China, India, Vietnam).

Changing business schools

Gilbert Lenssen, Professor of International Management in Bruges, Warsaw, Leiden and academic adviser to CSR Europe

I have always viewed business organizations as microcosms of society and a good place for social innovation. Likewise, I have always felt that the business activities I was engaged with needed to be tuned in to the larger societal context to enable innovation at all.

Working as an 'intrapreneur' in business has always been a rewarding growth experience for me, both intellectually and spiritually. That carries on and reflects on my current responsibilities as a teacher and researcher.

The major challenge facing me is to make a significant change to higher education, especially business schools and schools of government in terms of new ways of innovative and interdisciplinary learning, with a view to helping young people gain a sense of unity and interdependency both in the 'outside' material world and the 'inside' spiritual world. I also feel a responsibility to ensure the enhancement of their sense of personal consciousness and responsibility as tomorrow's leaders.

SOLUTIONS AND STRATEGIES

I am taking risks by engaging in innovative teaching and research whilst retaining influence in the mainstream of academia, consulting and business. I am puzzled, like every other thinking person living in today's world of bewildering change, and I am making an honest effort to explore, find out and shape what comes next. I have no ready-made solutions or answers to all the questions.

On behalf of CSR Europe and TCC I co-ordinate the activities of a group of innovative academics from prominent European business schools, who want to break the mould in establishing the business case for Corporate Social Responsibility (CSR).

Researching and teaching a wider responsibility of business in society and a new relationship of business with government (at all levels, including global governance) will contribute to an understanding of the new (transmodern?) paradigm underlying the triangle of Business-Government-Society.

A distinctly European profile and role in the search for this new paradigm and its manifestation in business, government and society as well as in their mutual relationships might be possible. A new (European) social contract might emerge from this.

I will support CSR Europe, TCC, IBLF and the business schools from Cranfield, Ashridge, Copenhagen, ESADE/Barcelona and INSEAD in establishing a European Academy for CSR.

The Green Paper on CSR by the European Commission needs to be taken further (albeit in amended form) as a policy platform. Both CSR Europe and the College of Europe will be involved in this. The White Paper should propose interventions of intelligent 'light touch' government instead of old style regulation. CSR is a domain for new enterprise policy, not old style social policy.

RECOMMENDED ACTIONS

- Business schools should take the lead in redefining and clarifying the wider role of business in society and in government, and commit resources for groundbreaking research and development. EU R&D resources need to match these.
- Mainstream courses at business schools should adopt environmental, social and cultural considerations, parameters and criteria – in particular relating to corporate and business strategy, finance and accounting, human resource development, marketing, procurement and operations.
- Specialized seminars and optional courses on corporate citizenship

(rationale, strategies, implementation, monitoring) should be established or enhanced.

- Workshops on ethical and spiritual development, as well as enhanced historical and cultural understanding of contemporary challenges as *personal* challenges should be started at all business schools.
- The above actions apply to both MBA programmes and executive programmes.
- Business leaders, leaders of the investors' community and academic leaders should engage in a high level mutual dialogue resulting in high powered action research partnerships.
- New chairs in responsible business should be established.
- A European award for the best CSR inspired MBA programme should be launched.

Ethics, enterprise and development

Philippa Foster Back, Director of the Institute of Business Ethics

There is a need to embed the ethics or values of a company into its corporate culture if that company is going to fulfil its potential. This needs leadership from the top; recognition of the importance of a strategic head – walking the talk – to encourage stakeholder loyalty and, in particular, employee performance.

This may be summed up in the company's reputation and how it is perceived by others – bad companies ultimately fail. Enterprise and development need to be strategically sustainable, and if based on transparent and open values, will succeed. It is all about doing business ethically.

The biggest challenge is to overcome cynicism. There is also an urgent need to educate in schools and business schools the importance of values in business. There is an opportunity to raise awareness, as there is now a focus on company non-financial activities.

Some companies, as they openly address ethical issues, are benefiting as their reputations are enhanced, eg the oil companies such as BP and Shell.

The Institute of Business Ethics (IBE) is well placed to raise the awareness of these issues through discussion events and publications, training and encouraging companies to exchange experiences in a neutral, private forum.

The concept of values-driven business will help companies to develop sustainable policies of Corporate Social Responsibility that have meaning and will help foster an enterprise environment.

RECOMMENDATIONS

- Develop the common values across different sectors of society, government, business and NGOs.
- Using these as a base, ensure these values are introduced from an early age in the education process.
- Reinforce common values in the wider society through media communications.

The National Foundation for Teaching Entrepreneurship (NFTE)

Steve Alcock, Director

The National Foundation for Teaching Entrepreneurship is an international, non-profit organization founded in 1987, with its headquarters located in New York. NFTE-UK was incorporated as a company in July 2000 and attained status as a registered charity in November 2000. The NFTE is also represented in Belgium and Austria.

The NFTE is an academic and life skills curriculum that teaches young people business start-up skills by developing a range of key entrepreneurial competencies. The programme is supported by a full range of teacher and student materials, including a new internet based self-teaching programme, *Biz Tech*, developed and sponsored by Microsoft exclusively for the NFTE.

The NFTE places particular emphasis on reintegrating socially excluded and disaffected young people by offering an incentive to personal development by linking learning to making money and integrating the different components of the curriculum into an interdisciplinary project.

SUCCESSFUL SOLUTIONS AND STRATEGIES

- To encourage young people to take control of their own learning and development.
- To involve all students in 'Enterprise Learning' at a much earlier age in the school education system.
- To develop management and leadership styles in education that involve

pursuing opportunities without regard to resource limitations currently controlled.

● To develop in teachers and students an ability to think and act in a way that is opportunity-obsessed, holistic in approach and management orientated.

RECOMMENDATIONS FOR IMPLEMENTING THE STRATEGY

● Promote education in schools to develop the key entrepreneurial competencies (in both teachers and students) of communication, numeracy, literacy, problem solving, information management, business knowledge and IT in a practical, self-empowering way.

● Establish an entrepreneurial vision for Europe by committing to a policy of entrepreneurial literacy and promoting entrepreneurship as an essential part of citizenship development.

● Simplify legal and tax frameworks to encourage young people to implement their enterprise initiatives.

Finally, a quote from Michelle Araujo, an NFTE graduate who enrolled to the NFTE programme as a teenage mother of three children and now, ten years later, is running her own small business and is a highly productive member of her community. Michelle summarized the vision of many young people today when she said: 'My dream is not to die in poverty but to have poverty die in me.'

Developing new public sector competencies

Greg Parston, Office for Public Management

It is clear that the constitution and capacities of existing public sector organization in the UK cannot fully meet the public's need for public services. The public sector ethos of serving communities remains strong. There is a real sense that public sector organizations are not only different in value-base from private, for-profit organizations (with which they are vying to provide public services), but that they must stand opposed to the private sector's entry into the field. Yet, recent research has shown that there is both confusion within the public's mind about what makes a public service public and less concern about who provides the services than that the service is of high quality. All of this combines to demand public service organizations that are enterprising and that can encourage management to act entrepreneurially to meet consumer needs. However, this needs to be balanced with a recognition that the public believes that public money should not be diverted from services into shareholder profit.

Some organizations, such as Aquaterra Leisure in London and Newcastle City Council, have pushed the boundaries of public service organization to provide services in innovative ways. But, as we move to increase the private funding of core public services, such as health and education, it is clear that new competencies are also required to ensure that the creation of public good is the main priority. Public sector organizations need now to build on the prevailing public sector ethos while developing new forms and behaviours that enable services to be delivered in ways that best meet customer needs.

NEEDS, OPPORTUNITIES AND CHALLENGES

- Public sector management needs to be freed of the imposition of centrally formulated performance targets in order to respond to changing needs at local level.
- Public sector management needs to be allowed discretion and tolerance to work in more creative and entrepreneurial ways to achieve improved social outcomes.
- Public service organizations need freedom from political interference in operations while conforming to explicit political accountability.

SUCCESSFUL SOLUTIONS AND STRATEGIES

- Public service providers guarantee the primary aims of producing public (ie social) value – not shareholder value – over time.
- Income and thus additional resources can be generated from trading related to the delivery of services.
- Providers are able to raise capital in conventional markets – ie not only through central finance.
- Organizational efficiency and effectiveness is promoted through incentives related to managerial autonomy and not simply to performance-related pay.
- Public service organization can be explicitly held to account by different stakeholders, including the public.

Facilitating sustainable European investment in Asia

Philippe Bergeron, Director, Regional Institute of Environmental Technology

Investment is critical. It is the heartbeat of economic development. Without investment, capacity cannot be increased. It allows advances in productivity and enables the transfer of technology. It is also essential for the creation of employment opportunities. Countries with open investment regimes tend to have higher rates of growth and more rapidly decreasing poverty.

Although investment and trade are two sides of the same coin, investment is better able to leverage sustainable development. The non-trade impacts of the multilateral trade regime make global trade increasingly controversial and possibly incompatible with key sustainability principles such as the 'precautionary', the 'proximity' or the 'subsidiarity' principles. Free trade often adds unsustainable pressure on the natural resources of weakly regulated developing countries. Also, multilateral trade negotiations have unbalanced, top-down bias that tends to increase the rights of multinational corporations, while restricting the ability of government to act. This goes against the policy of flexibility needed by countries to pursue their own differentiated development interest by attracting selective foreign investment.

Investments, domestic or foreign, fall into four categories: resource seeking investment that extracts natural resources; market seeking investment that serves a local market; efficiency seeking investment that helps build economy of scale and lower production costs; and asset seeking Foreign Portfolio Investment (FPI) that enhances financial return of capital assets beyond their operative management. Of these, resource, market or efficiency seeking investments (especially Foreign Direct Investments – FDI) tend to be a more stable source of finance compared to other forms of international capital flow, and globally dwarf overseas development aid as a source of finance for development in emerging countries.

A sustainable investment is an investment that helps meet people's 'essential' needs. It can address a wide range of economic sectors like healthy food, clean water, clean air, bio-diversity, mobility, clean and renewable energy, health care, built environment, closed-loop industry, learning, leisure, communication etc. In striving to satisfy a triple bottom line (economic prosperity, environmental sustainability and social equity), a sustainable investment has superior underlying economic fundamentals and is therefore expected to generate higher return. More significantly, it can help reach out to a broader base of potential customers, accelerate the alleviation of poverty, promote social justice and reduce waste, inefficiency and risk.

The difficulty resides in defining a sustainable investment. It cannot be prescribed by a set of fixed criteria or specifications. It is a perpetually moving target with characteristics that depend on levels of economic development, socio-cultural values and more importantly changing 'sustainability' risks as perceived by stakeholders. Defining sustainable investment requires a relentless engagement and debate with all the stakeholders who share benefits and losses from this investment to ensure that widely accepted triple bottom line criteria are sustained. An investment can best be labelled as sustainable when, through periodic multi-stakeholder scrutiny and monitoring, it succeeds to balance economic, environmental, social and local community aspects and impacts.

With large western institutional investors (pension funds, insurances etc) under growing regulatory pressure to report publicly on the 'sustainability' impact of their investment policies, it is expected that the demand for sustainable investment will grow significantly and rapidly in the future.

To serve this emerging demand, it is proposed to develop a new networking tool for government, business, finance, research and civil society to foster border-crossing dialogue and track knowledge about investments and their sustainability in line with the triple bottom line. As Asia is expected to attract a major share of future global FDI, while facing increasingly severe triple bottom line imbalance, it is proposed to test case the network there.

Tentatively called Asia e^3 INVEST (with e^3 standing for **e**conomic prosperity, **e**nvironmental sustainability and social **e**quity and INVEST for **I**nternational **N**etwork for **V**ibrant and **E**mpowering **S**ustainable **T**ransformation), the network is expected to:

- act as a forum for investment information and project exchange and mediation
- operate as a think-tank to provide insight on evolving investment criteria, risk and facilitating mechanisms
- be an observatory of all kinds of investments in Asia and review their alignment with sustainability indicators
- train decision-makers on investment management and governance practices
- support triple bottom line bench-marking of investment
- publish sustainable investment guidebooks, directories and best practices.

To be able to deliver, Asia e^3 INVEST will mobilize the support and participation of five key categories of partners (public authority, finance and investor, industry and business, research and academia, and civil society). The focus of attention and action will be investments in three dimensions: economic and industrial sectors (industry, urban, infrastructure, services etc), investment types (resource seeking, market seeking, efficiency seeking and asset seeking), and investment flow types (domestic, South-South, East-West).

The value of establishing the network could be far reaching. It would help Asian developing countries leap-frog through more efficient investments. It would provide an attractive channel to tackle Asian poverty in an economic co-operation mode. It would help redress past serious regional triple bottom line imbalance.

By focusing on investment, especially FDI for which many Asian countries aggressively compete, Asia e³ INVEST would offer many benefits. Among others, it would improve international investment policy and decision-making practices and attract intellectual leadership at the highest policy-making level on key issues of economic development (innovation, productivity, entrepreneurship, risk, finance, governance, social responsibility etc).

For Asian industrialists, Asia e³ INVEST would facilitate access to a marketing and project mediation network on the supply and demand side of investment, enable triple bottom line bench-marks and provide access to advanced investment development services like management, technology, legal, accounting etc.

Third Sector Barter

John Theaker, Director

Thirdsectorbarter.net seeks to establish a global information, communication, goods, services and time exchange designed to aid the work and ethos of people and organizations in the fields of philanthropy, civil society and the non-profit sector (the so called 'Third Sector') throughout the world, whose aims are to support social justice and environmental sustainability.

In this respect this project concerns itself with three key overlapping issue areas:

- The Third Sector operates in the heart of society developing social capital based on trust, norms and networks that make the society we live in today possible. This continues despite the fact that all too often this kind of activity is overlooked by the monetary system. Dr Hazel Henderson talks about these aspects of society as the 'Love Economy' of unaccounted production, co-operation, community service, sharing, barter and mutual aid upon which the monetary sector relies.

- Corporate Citizenship is now rising up the agendas of a number of private companies. Many have signed up to the UN Global Compact, launched by Secretary General Kofi Annan at Davos in 1999, which promoted nine principles of corporate responsibility for protecting human and workers' rights and the environment. More companies are thinking about corporate citizenship strategically, integrating objectives across all functions of the business, knowing that these practices will be important to their long-term business success.

- Greening the economic activities of aligned consumers. There are tens of millions of people, perhaps billions, who consciously aspire to participate in a more sustainable and just world. Currently, even the most committed of this constituency (including most Third Sector organizations) are largely directing their economic activities to and through companies that are contributing to the world's problems, including (and in particular)the increasing transfer of wealth from those with less to those who already have more, and the discounting of, and devastation to, the habitat that supports life on the planet.

CURRENT NEEDS, CHALLENGES AND OPPORTUNITIES

- Technical challenge – to establish the best possible non-cash exchange process from a large array of possibilities, that will be based on the values and ethos of the non-profit sector. In addition to find suitable technological platforms.
- Business challenge – to obtain the necessary seed funding and frame a financially self-sustaining operation that is based in the non-profit sector.
- Organizational challenge – to launch a system that provides an international network of aligned groups.
- Opportunities – to develop a groundbreaking system that represents a really exciting opportunity to support the core principles of sustainable human development on many levels, including providing an alternative to the prevailing financial system, and by being a useful service to the many organizations and companies that are trying so hard to develop social justice and environmental sustainability.

SPECIFIC RECOMMENDATIONS FOR IMPLEMENTING THE STRATEGY

- Building the case for complementary currencies across Europe and currency reform in general – let's widen the euro debate to include awareness building about the importance of financial reform.

Remembering that the mainstream monetary process all too often destroys community and social capital (and the environment) in fostering competition and growth, whilst complementary currencies can foster co-operative efforts towards sustainability and social justice, we need to find ways that ordinary people can really change their basic consumptive habits through alternative exchange mechanisms.

- Building the awareness that the Third Sector now constitutes the leading arena for change and development, taking the centre stage of the work to protect and develop social capital, social justice and environmental sustainability. This could be primarily due to the realization that the private and public sectors are, on a very fundamental level, failing to satisfy the basic needs of both material and spiritual satisfaction, in the context of respecting and cherishing the world in which we live. Is it for this reason that PricewaterhouseCoopers send their managers to the Findhorn Foundation in an attempt to 'take the psycho-spiritual and emotional maturity of their employees as seriously as their intellectual ability'? In any event, forging ever stronger links at all levels between all three sectors will be necessary to ensure the vital growth of society.

- Following on from the above, seeking to develop management expertise within the Third Sector and find suitable mechanisms for assessing the viability and success of work being carried out will be vital, if the sector is to develop further.

Transparency International

FL Cockcroft, Founder

Tackling corruption as a threat to fair markets and even political stability within the EU and the ten 'accession' countries of Eastern Europe is of paramount importance. In the 1990s corruption emerged as a global phenonomenon and not one which is restricted to the 'South'. The dramatic cases identified in Italy in the mid-1990s, the prosecution of a one-time Secretary General of NATO on charges associated with the payment of bribes, and the extensive scandals surrounding Elf all serve to illustrate the problem within the EU itself. Much of this relates to the funding of political parties and expected pay-offs, with deep repercussions for the political system as has occurred in Germany. However, corruption can also impact at the level of the SME and form a barrier to the development of companies on this scale: this is particularly the case in 'accession countries'. Finally, bad practice within the EU regularly spills over into its relationship with the developing world through the payment of bribes to countries considering major infrastructure projects and the like.

Although major reforms to laws governing corruption have been made within the EU and by its member states in broader contexts in the last few years (eg the EU Convention on Corruption, the Council of Europe Criminal Law Convention on Corruption and the OECD Convention on Combating the Bribery of Public Officials), these have yet to be fully applied or even recognized and understood within the business community. Furthermore, there is a lack of cohesion within and between member states as to the most effective follow-up investigative and prosecutorial arrangements. The addition of anti-terrorist measures, however necessary, may have created a context in which corruption has become less important from the viewpoint of investigating authorities.

Much depends on the effective implementation of the above conventions and the associated legislation at national level. However, there is a major need for the adoption of corporate integrity systems that go well beyond codes of conduct and ensure real compliance at the level of the parent company, the subsidiary and joint venture partners. The latter particularly applies to the operations of EU-based companies in accession countries, other transition economies and the countries linked to the EU by the Cotonou Convention. Further, the development finance insitutions associated with the EU could go much further in ensuring that their funding does not support forms of corruption either directly or indirectly.

SPECIFIC RECOMMENDATIONS FOR IMPLEMENTING THE STRATEGY

- Full co-operation at the level of local and national governments.
- Full recognition by larger companies (especially those with operations in more than one member state, and in accession and African–Caribbean and Pacific – ACP – countries) of the significance of their operations for the fight against corruption.
- Effective collaboration between investigative agencies fighting corruption – not yet achieved, though much heralded.
- Full acceptance by development finance insitutions of their responsibilities.
- Active collaboration between TI chapters (both within the EU and in accession countries) and development of a stonger common policy position re developments within the EU Commission and Parliament (the new EU Corporate Responsibility Initiative is a case in point).

The Work Research Foundation – a national coalition for working life and organizational competence

Richard Ennals, Peter Totterdill and Campbell Ford, Directors of the Work Research Foundation, UK

Despite its early contributions to the development of working life research, the UK has lagged behind much of the rest of Northern Europe in establishing a coherent approach to the modernization of work organization. The removal of tripartite structures by the Thatcher and Major governments and their decision to opt out of significant areas of European employment policy left the UK ill-prepared to respond to emerging economic or policy challenges in Europe. Evidence of an increasing gap between leading-edge practice and common practice in UK workplaces has emerged forcibly as a key issue for future productivity and employment.

The UK Work Organisation Network (UK WON) was first established in 1996 as a coalition between researchers, business support organizations and social partners, slowly building a portfolio of projects designed to support workplace innovation. More recently the creation of the Work Research Foundation (WRF), a partnership-based company with responsibility for managing the activities of the Network, firmly establishes UK WON as a significant vehicle for social dialogue and organizational change.

More information on UK WON and the WRF can be found at www.ukwon.net

Appendix 2

Attendees to the European Enterprise Summit 4–5 November 2001, The Industrial Society (now known as The Work Foundation), 3 Carlton House Terrace, London, and members of the European Enterprise Network

Steve Alcock – the National Foundation for Teaching Entrepreneurship

Wendy Alexander – [former] Minister for Enterprise, Lifelong Learning and Transport, the Scottish Executive

Dr Agni Vlavianos-Arvanitis – the Biopolitics International Organisation

Philippa Foster Back – Institute of Business Ethics

Tom Bentley – Demos

Philippe Bergeron – Regional Institute of Environmental Technology

Georges Berthoin – Hon European President of Tri-lateral Commission, European Movement

Theo Blackwell – The Industrial Society (now known as The Work Foundation)

Lawrence Bloom – international entrepreneur

Charles Bodwell – the Management and Corporate Citizenship Programme, ILO

Stephen Brenninkmeyer – the National Foundation for Teaching Entrepreneurship

Jermyn Brooks – PwC

Patrick Burns – The Industrial Society (now known as The Work Foundation)

Cari Caldwell – PriceWaterhouseCoopers

Tom Cannon – RespectLondon

Alan Christie – Levi Strauss

FL Cockcroft – Transparency International

Rosalind Copisarow – UnLtd

Diane Coyle – Enlightenment Economics

Ged Davis – Shell

Maarten De Pous – the Caux Round Table, Netherlands

Stephanie Draper – The Industrial Society (now known as The Work Foundation)

Nick Dunlop – Earth Action UK

Malcolm Ehrenpreis – World Bank counsellor for UK

Bo Ekman – Nextwork

John Elkington – SustainAbility

Kaj Embrén – RespectEurope

Memuna Forna – The Industrial Society (now known as The Work Foundation)

Claude Fussler – the World Business Council for Sustainable Development

Jim Garrison – the State of the World Forum

Professor Anthony Giddens – LSE

David Grayson – Business in the Community

Robert Harrison – McKinsey

Erica Hauver – social involvement consultant

Hazel Henderson – author, partner Calvert-Henderson Quality of Life Indicators, USA

Tony Hoskins – the Virtuous Circle

Will Hutton – The Industrial Society (now known as The Work Foundation)

Nick Isles – The Industrial Society (now known as The Work Foundation)

Peter Johnston – the European Commission

Richard Jolly – StokesJolly

Annette Kleinfeld – the European Business Ethics Network (EBEN)

Paul Kloppenburg – Progressio Foundation

John Knell – The Industrial Society (now known as The Work Foundation)

Elisabeth Laville – Utopies

Gilbert Lenssen – College of Europe, Bruges

Vergilio Levaggi – the ILO

Maria Cattaui Livanos – the International Chamber of Commerce

Josep M Lozano – ESADE
Jens Erik Lund – Social Ministeriet, Denmark
Marc Luyckx – Vision 2020
Ermanno Magnani – Fondazione Rispetto e Parita
Ed Mayo – the New Economics Foundation
Melina Mehra – Centre for Social Markets
Lars Mortensen – the Kaos Pilots, Denmark
Geoff Mulgan – the Cabinet Office
Jeremy Oppenheim – McKinsey, Chair of UnLtd, the UK Foundation for
    Social Entrepreneurs
Marcello Palazzi – Progressio Foundation
Greg Parston – the Office for Public Management
Tanya Pein – the Accelerator Group
John Philpott – the Chartered Institute of Personnel and Development
Tom Rautenberg – the State of the World Forum
Dr Martin Ridge – the DTI
Robert Rubinstein – Brooklyn Bridge
Philip Sadler – Tomorrow's Company
Susan Simpson – Prince of Wales Business Leaders' Forum
Alan Sinclair – Scottish Enterprise, former head of Wise Group
Rt Hon Andrew Smith MP – Chief Secretary to the Treasury
Juan Somavia – the International Labour Organization
Tom Spencer – the European Centre for Public Affairs
George Starcher – the European Baha'I Business Forum
Sir Sigmund Sternberg
Chris Tchen – Strategos
John Theaker – Third Sector Barter
Peter Totterdill – the Work Research Foundation
Daniel Truran – Progressio Foundation
Colin Tweedy and Philip Spedding – Arts &Business
Raymond Van Ermen – European Partners for the Environment (EPE)
Marc Van Der Erve – Evolution Management
Geert Van Maanen – Oikocredit, NL
Alice Verroen – Progressio Foundation

Claudia Von Monbart – the World Bank
Jan Oluf Willums – Inspire-Norway
Andrew Wilson – Ashridge Centre for Business and Society
Jean-Pierre Worms – Laboratory of the Future
Nick Wright – UBS Warburg
Simon Zadek – the Institute of Social and Ethical Accountability

Appendix 3

Outcomes note from the European Enterprise Summit, London 4–5 November 2001

1. INTRODUCTION

The Progressio Foundation, The Industrial Society (now known as The Work Foundation) and the State of the World Forum welcomed over 80 leading thinkers, activists, business leaders and policy advisers to The Industrial Society's central London headquarters on 4 November for 24 hours of discussion, debate and agenda setting on the subject of developing a progressive European enterprise strategy.

The focus of the discussions over the period was on how to scale-up the myriad activities already being undertaken by many of those present into the more coherent development of a progressive enterprise strategy that would have greater impact both in Europe and globally.

The consensus of the summit was that although a major challenge, Europe did indeed have much to offer the world in terms of lessons in institution building, developing a progressive form/s of market capitalism and the ongoing quest to reform that capitalism in order to ensure it is truly innovative, accountable and embedded in notions of excellence, social justice and inclusiveness.

The summit threw up many ideas and suggestions for further development which are summarized below.

The event was framed by a strategy document that offered a draft agenda, summing up what a progressive European enterprise strategy might look like in the broadest terms. After brief discussion of this document the summit moved on to developing answers to eight core questions. These were:

- What are the major constraints for change?
- What is the action plan for business?
- What is the action plan for civil society?
- What is the action plan for governments?
- How should business, civil society and government act in an integrated way?
- What are the possible new organizational forms?
- What are the successful processes that have been used to achieve change?
- What are the best practices/best European models?

Finally, the summit was asked to identify five key action points in answer to each question. These points are listed in full below.

2. KEY COMMENTS ON DRAFT STRATEGY DOCUMENT (SEE APPENDIX 4 FOR ORIGINAL TEXT)

It was recognized by the summit that the draft strategy document could lead to a process of defining what might be included in an Enterprise Chapter, agreed at EU-level as part of the Intergovernmental Conference of the European Union in 2004. One group suggested that the purpose of the document should be to explore the extent to which the tradition and evolving dimensions of enterprise in Europe, both in society at large and in business corporations, can be strengthened and developed to a greater role both in the EU itself and in the process of globalization in order to improve the quality and continuity of life. The positive aspects of globalization should be iterated as part of the preamble.

There was however no attempt made to agree the document as part of the summit discussions, but rather to see it as representing the broad agenda, which along with the plenary presentations would feed into the summit process.

In defining an enterprise strategy the need for a new common language was identified, a language that was inclusive, not necessarily western in derivation and that emphasized the importance of dialogue.

Any strategy document needed to make clear what corporates need to do to develop better business practices, perhaps using a sub-heading such as 'helping business to make a bigger contribution' or 'helping business and society work together'. The key is to understand that businesses are social actors that interact with other social actors. Companies are not self-sufficient.

The emphasis should be on *enterprise* rather than Europe since enterprise is global and needs to be seen as that. The goal of strategy at a European level must be to define the model and then work with European institutions at a policy level.

European enterprise was born out of conflict and an understanding of that history is required in order to apply the lessons learned at a global level.

It is important to guard against the document becoming a manifesto that ignores the flaws in the European model and erodes the value of such a document, reducing it to the status of a 'political football'.

The focus in future should be on clarifying the micro-implications of these principles and establishing more empirical evidence about the validity of some of our assumptions.

There needs to be more in such a document on the organization of labour and how to create workplaces that enable people to use their full creative potential.

3. PRÉCIS OF MAIN DISCUSSION

Taking the eight questions listed above, the ensuing discussions were wide-ranging and full of ideas. The group looking at the constraints for change identified the need to focus on key levers in order to move the agenda forward. Short-term investment flows that destabilize economies and act against sustainability were identified as a major constraint on developing a more inclusive, long-term stakeholder orientated business model.

A lack of unanimity among NGOs was also seen as hampering the development of a rational countervailing argument to the Washington consensus in international dialogues.

Finally, a third group of comments focused on the need to improve higher education systems – in particular business school syllabuses.

The group looking at what business should do focused considerable attention on fast tracking high-fliers and other groups, such as chief financial officers, into contact with grass-roots entrepreneurs and enterprise initiatives, together with efforts to refocus these individuals' ethical outlook. Hand-in-hand with these types of approaches aimed at the individual business leader, was a focus on mobilizing the power of the investment community to drive change around the CSR agenda. In order to persuade business of the need for change, better measurement of the impact of more ethical business performance was recognized as being necessary in order to make the business case irrefutable.

In summary, the following issues were identified as key: engagement with the tipping points that will generate the critical mass necessary to change business thinking and practices (companies need to feel more pain); building the business case; working with key business leaders; engendering entrepreneurship as a core value throughout European society; capturing and expanding the experiments with the reporting of intangibles as part of the new accounting; building the pressure for 'hard' CSR through naming and shaming, and using social capital as a business resource.

On civil society, the core actions were focused on developing a more coherent narrative alongside the need to re-enchant people through recognizing the power that people, either individually or collectively, have. Suggestions included a global tax on advertising to fund consumer literacy and the recognition that government needs to accelerate the processes of change rather than merely try and control them (ie slow them down). The media also needs to be freed up to reflect alternative dialogues – South-North rather than North-South.

For governments the challenge was seen to be to engage in more mature dialogue with companies. They need to invest in proving the business benefits of 'hard' CSR, taking into account regional and cultural diversity. They also need to create the environment in which companies are able to be transparent and communicate by improving the information available to the public by reports, better labelling etc.

Every European government should also have a minister responsible for CSR. For Europe, the feeling was that action is a question of political will rather than institutional change. The integration of the European model must not mean creating a European economic fortress but an example capable of replication at a global level, whereby Europe has the opportunity of being at the epicentre of redefining the prevailing model of market capitalism. One suggestion was for a European New Deal as a short-term response to getting through the global downturn and managing enlargement.

However, the meeting noted the success of existing processes. The Danish and Dutch Governments' involvement in building CSR initiatives was cited on several occasions.

Max Havelaar and The Body Shop were also mentioned as examples of moving public opinion and consensus towards a different way of doing business. The Danish windmill industry, Tetrapak, Unilever and Fabergé were also mentioned as having developed ways of doing business that had created new models of involvement with other stakeholders.

4. MAIN CONCLUSIONS AND ACTION POINTS

Recorded below are the conclusions of the final session of the summit from which next steps will be built.

WHAT ARE THE MAJOR CONSTRAINTS FOR CHANGE?
- The fact that breakthrough tends to require a context of crisis.
- Western self-interest and complacency about wealth/resource disparity.
- Lack of unanimity and focused countervailing opinion among NGOs.
- Over-concentration on old paradigms and failure to focus on critical new systems and levers for change.
- Failure to listen to and include the disadvantaged in international dialogue and micro-initiatives.

WHAT IS THE ACTION PLAN FOR BUSINESS?
- Needs to be partly a process of political leadership – business leaders engaged in political debate in Europe.

- The need for engagement with the reality of organizational life – incentives to change are, at best, mixed.
- New models need to be created in practice as well as in theory – creating networks of innovators across businesses, not just at the tops of businesses.
- Measuring progress differently is fundamental and has to be developed further.
- Creativity in society rests on a broader definition and value of entrepreneurship.

WHAT IS THE ACTION PLAN FOR CIVIL SOCIETY?

- Purist definition: voluntary, citizen-based, not-for-profit organizations working for the common good.
- The current system of values and organizations leads to an unsustainable future.
- Whenever we trust the new values inside ourselves we re-enchant ourselves. This is the energy of the future civil society, eg the Global Public Access Television network; Jubilee 2000.
- Action plan: to make the media socially responsible by, for example, introducing a tax on advertising which is used to promote consumer literacy. The media needs to be opened up to new values and new actors in order to shift from the unsustainable paradigm.
- Mainstreaming serendipity and grass-roots creativity; building a high impact civil society.

WHAT IS THE ACTION PLAN FOR GOVERNMENT?

- Take steps to harmonize and share CSR practices across Europe, taking account of regional and cultural diversity. Government has a role in facilitating productive debate within the business community on the principles of CSR.
- Recognize that government affects business at different levels, by different means, eg from legislation to exhorting good CSR practices. Government should look at new ways to incentivize CSR, eg via

procurement, recognition programmes, supporting research to justify the business case for CSR – to convert the unconverted.

- Ensure clear ministerial responsibility for CSR, raise the profile of the minister. Responsibilities to include legislation relating to CSR, and perhaps even a budget for internal CSR practices and ensuring that internal CSR practices are to an acceptable standard. Government to act as 'role models' to other countries and multinational organizations.

- To create the environment in which companies are able to be transparent and communicate widely with government, NGOs and others, eg improving the information available to the public by reports, better labelling etc. Ensure that companies and public sector bodies are 'allowed to fail' as part of the learning process.

- Improve understanding of CSR, ethical consumption etc via education programmes for individuals of all ages.

- Government has a role in creating an environment of social cohesion/inclusion that can be understood and actioned in partnership with business.

INTEGRATED ACTION PLAN – BUSINESS, CIVIL SOCIETY AND GOVERNMENT?

- Focus on a few key things that emerge from this summit and bench-mark and target work, eg business schools.

- Let's get socially responsible entrepreneurialism on the Education agenda both at secondary school and business school level.

- Create multiple platforms for dialogue across groups that are not normally in contact. Be able to think the unthinkable and the unfashionable.

- Encourage more platforms to create understanding, eg internet, face to face, tri-sectoral. Think about the power that we have in creating practical ways forward.

- Fulfil our own responsibilities.

- Harness the institutional investment communities, eg target your pension fund trustee.

WHAT ARE POSSIBLE NEW ORGANIZATIONAL FORMS?

- Encourage new organizational forms through the promotion of ethical reporting/management systems.
- Examine and reform the institutional framework for social entrepreneurs.
- Appraise and reform the structure of trusts, charities and foundations to empower them under different national systems to invest and support socially responsible enterprises.
- Pension fund trustees to declare ethical and social objectives, as suggested in CSR Green Paper.
- The Commission to encourage information dissemination/best practice amongst social entrepreneurs across member states via national action plans and an 'ideas bank'.
- Promote partnerships between sectors – establishing innovative bidding mechanisms to encourage better partnerships between public, private and voluntary sectors.

WHAT ARE THE SUCCESSFUL PROCESSES THAT HAVE BEEN USED TO ACHIEVE CHANGE?

- Involved but intelligent government intervention making full use of stakeholders' abilities in order to create a consensus environment, eg Dutch, Scandinavian cultures. But will such interventions work in Latin cultures? Using the tax system to achieve change, eg the solar system in Holland and windmills in Denmark.
- Create transparency both internally and externally with all stakeholders. Create rules for transparency and for audit, specifying criteria, measuring in time, eg La Farge involving the WWF, the World Bank. Also Shell sustainability report.
- Body Shop example of communicating concepts and not just products, creating trust in them. Max Havelaar identified key consumers prepared to pay more for socially responsible business, which has led to business innovation.
- Involve the arts and innovation in marketing, making use of their inherent creativity to express feelings and create change.

- Promote role models/best practice/innovation/'heroes'/visions of the future, using the press. Acknowledge progress, creativity and innovation through awards. Put on record what the best practices are.
- All stakeholders in society, including businesses, should have a permanent open dialogue between consciousness and human development and the use of capital and traditional business practices.

WHAT ARE THE BEST PRACTICES/BEST EUROPEAN MODELS?

- More democratic global institutions are needed to create incentives for companies to change.
- More accessible information and greater transparency needed so consumers can monitor corporate behaviour.
- There are many examples of best practice – not just one European model to be copied elsewhere – these need to be underpinned by values such as transparency, compliance, positive screening.
- Challenges: to find ways to build relationships between the different sectors and find better ways for stakeholder dialogues.
- We must communicate the agenda better and translate the jargon.

5. INITIAL FUTURE ACTIONS

There were several levels of activity identified at the summit. Initial follow-up ideas were as follows:

1. Arrange bi-lateral meetings with the European Commission and ILO.
2. Develop the agenda discussed at the summit through separate smaller meetings and working groups in different European centres. These meetings would also act as a way of enlarging the network prior to the next major summit in 2003.
3. Develop the ideas around a research agenda whose common theme is defining and better measurement of the European enterprise model.
4. Plan for a larger Davos-style summit in 2003 that will require major financial and logistical support from members of the network and others.

Appendix 4
Agenda for a European progressive enterprise chapter

1. Globalization is not an immutable force. It is capable of being shaped and developed. The future of globalization should be dependent on it being bounded by law and justice and offering opportunities that will benefit the many and not just the few. Globalization's goal over the next few years should be to develop a model of market capitalism that is equitable and redistributive, vigorously anti-poverty and capable of including all the world's population in a way that is democratic and accountable, respectful of human rights and environmentally sustainable.

2. European enterprise should be based on core values and concepts. It should be high productivity, high performance enterprise. Its agenda encompasses the broad areas of social enterprise, just economic policies, high ethical, environmental and human standards, ethical investment, access to micro-credit, a sustainable public procurement programme, a transparent transaction regime, an ethical trading regime and new forms of public interest companies. The culture of European enterprise offers a beacon to help drive the building of new global institutions designed to entrench democratic processes, develop an understanding of human rights and encourage efficient systems that manage the global environment in a sustainable manner and that enable and support competition and a market economy.

3. There are a number of core building blocks of a common European enterprise strategy. First, education is key to establishing the enterprise agenda, building a new culture and ensuring common values are understood by future generations. It offers wealth to the developing world, and international competitiveness to Europe; it is the source of

economic growth, and the basis of a rich and ethical human culture.

4. Socially responsible companies are more profitable, growth enhancing, wealth creating, socially desirable and ethical. As a minimum, companies should disclose publicly how their functioning impacts society, should obey the law and exercise restraint in influencing and financing government. Companies need to incorporate the OECD guidelines for companies explicitly in their practice. A core fundamental is to realize that shareholders can no longer be preferred over other stakeholders. Adopting 'hard' Corporate Social Responsibility measures should be a goal of all European enterprise.

5. The process of delivering accountability to stakeholders unlocks entrepreneurialism by providing access to stakeholder perspectives and building organizational capacity from such new sources of knowledge. Improving organizational accountability should be part of learning for entrepreneurs and business leaders at all levels of the education process. Organizations that encourage accountability measures should be recognized. The investment community needs to be drawn into the debate as a key influencer. Governments, employer bodies and the wider community need to recognize 'best of' corporate social enterprise initiatives and encourage their spread.

6. Corporate restructuring should follow clear principles that seek to minimize disruption, harm to local communities, damage to the future employment prospects of laid-off workers and the rupturing of supply chain relationships.

7. European enterprise recognizes that organizations work best when they manage their workforces through high trust relationships, are committed to diversity in all its dimensions and create a balance between stakeholder interests. High levels of information exchange and consultation are a non-negotiable building block in developing such high trust relationships. Commitment to service in the widest sense is the key value that informs business decisions and drives loyalty. It is not about buying cheap and selling dear.

8. European enterprise recognizes that all organizations, whether large or small, are bound by the 'new fundamentals' that acknowledge the reality of global warming, climate change and the need to protect and

conserve the environment. The 'new fundamentals' mean that there is a recognition of the need to move beyond the concept of sustainability towards forms of global environmental legislation and bio-economics, which redefine the concept of profit and recognize the role of 'human obligations' alongside the well established idea of human rights. European governments should integrate the concept of a 'Green Salary' into their respective unemployment strategies and place work that enhances the environment at the heart of such strategies. An active European Court of the Environment should be established as soon as possible.

9. A European enterprise agenda will only work through an integrated approach that encourages innovations and strategies at all levels. It needs to distinguish what is best done at the European, national, regional, community and individual levels. Government regulation has a clear role to play in this and elsewhere in the strategy. A core building block of the Enterprise strategy is to sustain the rapid deployment of high speed network access in every community.

10. Reform of the current financial system is a critical element in building a more inclusive form of market capitalism. New forms of taxation on consumption and environmental use are required. European enterprise values patient investors who maintain a long-term interest in the companies in which they invest. Alternative exchange and barter mechanisms also have an important role to play for micro-enterprises and communities.

11. The need to embed enterprise in high trust networks means that there must be a commitment to high quality urban life. An integrated global urban reconstruction strategy is needed that brings together social innovators, government departments, local associations and economic and financial institutions with empowered local communities. Social capital building will result if such integrated projects are delivered. In addition, European enterprise recognizes that thriving cultural industries are essential to communicating business values, encouraging entrepreneurialism and building social cohesion. To facilitate this dimension of the enterprise strategy a 'Davos for the Arts' is proposed.

12. European enterprise believes in a strong public infrastructure. Public

services exist to serve the public good. Innovations designed to improve the delivery, effectiveness and impact of public services will prove ineffective if this goal is lost. Public sector management must be capable of acting with flexibility and responding to needs as they arise. They must be allowed the discretion to be more creative and entrepreneurial in order to achieve improved social outcomes, while not losing accountability or transparency. Public service providers should be able to generate additional resources through trading, raise capital in conventional markets, offer other forms of incentives related to managerial autonomy and not simply performance related pay, and be accountable to a variety of stakeholders including the public.